Praise for *Executing Excellence*

"This collaborative work, curated by a team of highly accomplished project managers, educators, and writers, is an excellent guide for project management professionals. This book navigates complexities such as project authority, stress management, and the nuanced differences between *De Facto* and *De Jure* Projects.

"The team of writers addresses project success, freelancing dynamics, and integrating technology, including AI. It adeptly explores effective communication, the symbiosis of management and leadership, and essential elements like personal branding, value-driven performance, and diversity in project management. With a comprehensive approach encompassing communication, experience, mentoring, and emotional intelligence, this insightful guide is indispensable for project managers across diverse industries."

Joseph Phillips, PMP, PMI-ACP, PSM, Project+, CTT+
Director of Education, Instructing.com

"So much project wisdom packed into one guide. Whether you're a seasoned project pro or aspiring to move into this field, you'll walk away from this book with practical insights and ideas that will help you take the next step in your ability to lead and deliver."

Andy Kaufman
Host of the *People and Projects Podcast*

"This book is ground-breaking, as it combines input from some of the finest minds in the profession, leaving nothing to chance! Those just starting their journey are lucky to have such an amazing book as a 'real world' guide to achieving excellence! Impressive!"

Lee R. Lambert
PMI Fellow and a Founder of the PMP

Excecuting Excellence

Actionable Insights From 10 Savvy Project Managers

Adrian Dooley
Kayla McGuire
Dr. Tori R. Dodla
Dr. Max Boller
Joseph Jordan

Walt Sparling
Tareka Wheeler
John Connolly
Jeremiah Hammon
Mark Rozner

Foreword by
Terry Dean Schmidt

Community Milestone Press

Executing Excellence, copyright © 2024, Salientian, LLC, DBA Community Milestone Press.
Solving the Paradox of Project Success, copyright © 2024 Adrian Dooley.
Freelancing and Project Management, copyright © 2024 Kayla McGuire.
Tech-Forward Project Management: Mastering the Digital Landscape, copyright © 2024 Tori R. Dodla.
Project Manager Authority and the Affect It Has on Project Manager Stress, copyright © 2024 Max Boller.
De Facto *vs.* De Jure *Projects,* copyright © 2024 Joseph Jordan.
Good Communication Practices Throughout the Project Lifecycle, copyright © 2024 Walt Sparling.
From Manager to Leader: Unboxing the Power of Value-Based Performance and Personal Branding, copyright © 2024 Tareka Wheeler.
Lessons from Outside: Infinite Diversity in Infinite Combinations, copyright © 2024 John Connolly.
Emotional Intelligence for Project Managers: The Art of Managing Self to Connect with Others, copyright © 2024 Jeremiah Hammon.
Finding the Function in Dysfunction: Trauma's Impact on Project Management Leadership, copyright © 2024 Mark Rozner.

ISBN (Paperback): 979-8-9892418-0-4
ISBN (EPUB): 979-8-9892418-1-1
ISBN (Kindle): 979-8-9892418-2-8

All rights reserved. No part of this publication may be reproduced, stored in a retrieval system, or transmitted in any form or by any means, electronic, mechanical, recording or otherwise, without the prior written permission of the publisher, except by a reviewer who may quote brief passages in a review.

Body typeface: Sentient, licensed under the ITF Free Font License v. 1.0. Header typeface: Red Hat Display, licensed under the SIL Open Font License v. 1.1.

First Edition

For project managers everywhere

May you execute projects with excellence throughout your careers

Contents

Foreword: Execution Excellence	*xiii*
Introduction	*xxi*
Chapter One: Solving the Paradox of Project Success	1
Chapter Two: Freelancing and Project Management	21
Chapter Three: Tech-Forward Project Management: Mastering the Digital Landscape	37
Chapter Four: Project Manager Authority and the Affect It Has on Project Manager Stress	53
Chapter Five: *De Facto* vs. *De Jure* Projects	75
Chapter Six: Good Communication Practices Throughout the Project Lifecycle	91
Chapter Seven: From Manager to Leader: Unboxing the Power of Value-Based Performance and Personal Branding	109
Chapter Eight: Lessons from Outside: Infinite Diversity in Infinite Combinations	117
Chapter Nine: Emotional Intelligence for Project Managers: The Art of Managing Self to Connect with Others	131
Chapter Ten: Finding the Function in Dysfunction: Trauma's Impact on Project Management Leadership	149
Afterword	167
About the Authors	171

Foreword: Execution Excellence

By Terry Dean Schmidt, author of
Strategic Project Management Made Simple

It's not often that a Project Management focused book grabs my full attention. That's because over a five-decade international PM career, I've read nearly all of them. Most of these books rehash the same tired old themes.

That's why it's a pleasant surprise to come across a book that truly offers new ideas and fresh perspectives.

John Connolly has done a superb job of discovering and organizing a roster of amazing project managers and writers. Some are seasoned PMs; others are rising stars. But each one shares their heart-felt and experience-proven wisdom.

My sincere belief is that Project Managers like you are the unsung heroes of the word because they are responsible for 90 percent of progress in the world. Project Management is one of the greatest careers imaginable because of the variety of projects in which you can engage – and the difference you can make – once you master the basics.

Whether you're facing tough tasks or just want to learn more about managing projects, the ten essays that follow invite you to dive deep into the sea of new knowledge.

This book stands out as a beacon of high cross-field mobility for PMs. It shows how PM skills and principles can transcend traditional boundaries, applying across various industries and disciplines with ease.

Whether you are in tech, healthcare, construction, or just about any kind of knowledge work, the insights and strategies that follow are universally applicable.

As you proceed, look for those powerful ideas that could boost your skills and totally up-level your PM game. Get ready to discover those "aha" moments!

Here's a quick take on each chapter.

In *Solving the Paradox of Project Success* Adrian Dooley explores the root cause of Cobb's Paradox: "We know why projects fail; we know how to prevent their failure – so why do they still fail?" First, Adrian challenges the common "reasons" and identifies the barriers that stop the fundamentals being applied to project management effectively.

Next, Adrian introduces the Praxis Framework, a solution designed to overcome barriers. He then shared how future technology such as AI can help with good practice. Finally, he suggests, "if you make those basics a habit, then you can start to think about doing the clever stuff." Simple yet true. "Failure happens when you lose that foundation."

In *Freelancing and Project Management*, Kayla McGuire invites you to take a ride on her journey to explore how to become a freelance project manager. "All it takes is a vision, strategy, and consistent effort."

She begins her tips with the emphasis on a personal vision statement. "Once you have this figured out, start acting like this person today. This is the first step." She then presents three key skills you don't want to miss. You will learn how to "get comfortable with navigating the unknown;" you will read and learn from her networking mistakes. Enjoy this ride with Kayla!

In *Tech-Forward Project Management: Mastering the Digital Landscape,* Dr. Tori R. Dodla shares her first project management role experience at a hospital. "I suffered, and I suffered greatly." Learning from her mistakes, she shares six technology-driven recommendations and digital tools.

You will see why learning technical language is crucial to establish credibility and trust. You will find out why understanding each team member's workload can help you communicate more effectively. You will explore how to use technology to improve notetaking. "I never had enough time for anything, and I almost always forgot the little things." Sound familiar? Read the last tip to find the answer!

You know that old saying, "with great power comes great responsibility"? In *Project Manager Authority and the Effect It Has on Project Manager Stress,* Dr. Max Boller dives deep into the intricate relationship between a project manager's authority and the stress they content with. "It's empowering, no doubt, but it also means the project manager is the go-to person if things go south."

There's a bit of a double-edged sword. On one side, it gives project managers with the autonomy and flexibility, but on the flip side, it can crank up stress levels. The magic power, according to Dr. Max Boller, is to discover "the right balance". So read on, obtain the "secret weapon" and find the "sweet spot"!

Are you looking to transform some tasks into small projects? Or are you preparing yourself to register for the PMP certification exam? Nodding? Then this chapter is for you. In De Facto *vs.* De Jure *Projects,* Joesph Jordan first explains *de jure* and *de facto* projects. He then focuses on *de facto* projects and walks us through each process of planning, executing, and completing step.

What if the project was completed behind schedule and/or over budget? "Do not despair", says Joesph, "You take these lessons learned to do a better forecasting job next time. Practice leads to better performance – never to perfection."

"In the real estate world, an agent's mantra is location, location, location." Have you ever wondered what is the mantra in the project management world? Walt Sparling answered this question in *Good Communication Practices Throughout the Project Lifecycle*: "it is all about communication, communication, communication."

"Do you sometimes appear comfortable or confident, do you portray a lack of interest, or maybe even distrust?" Well, it's time to smooth out your rough edges. Sparling challenges you to face some of the hardest verbal communication skills anyone can master. And he dishes out some of the best practices used by outstanding project leaders.

In *From Manager to Leader: Unboxing the Power of Value-Based Performance and Personal Branding*, Tareka Wheeler encourages you to release the power of "value-based performance and personal branding."

"Success isn't just about delivering on time and within budget anymore." You may ask, so what else? "It's about value," she says. "Your performance is not about you. Your performance is about the value that you bring to all the stakeholders involved in your project."

Getting inspired? Keep reading and find practical strategies in this chapter. Learn to "accept opportunities to lead or support highly visible projects or initiatives and execute them in your unique way." Now it is your turn to lead and shine.

Step into John Connolly's world, where the Star Trek principle of "Infinite Diversity in Infinite Combinations" isn't just a cool space concept – it's the golden rule of project management! Having made the transition from "a librarian who manages projects" to "a project manager with a library background," John encourages newcomers to blast their unique background into the universe.

And to those who are already established in the field, Connolly suggests that you "both teach and learn from newcomers in equal measure." Get ready to be entertained and inspired in Lessons from Outside: Infinite Diversity in Infinite Combinations.

In *Emotional Intelligence for Project Managers: The Art of Managing Self to Connect with Others*, Jeremiah Hammon demonstrated the importance of Emotional Intelligence (EQ) for project managers. "EQ is not only good for your relationship, but also for you and everyone around you!"

Early in his career he discovered "the missing piece in my skill set: the ability to understand how I perceived and reacted in stressful situations." He shares what "triggers" dysfunctional emotions and ways to master self-awareness. You will find tips on how to develop your self-confidence and master your self-management. Time to boost your EQ to the next level as a leader.

In *Finding the Function in Dysfunction: Trauma's Impact on Project Management Leadership*, Mark Rozner guides us on turning trauma into strengths and opportunities for self-growth. This means taking the "bad" and turning it "good." He posits, "if you grew up in a state of chaos, neglect, or abuse, you have more than likely developed skills that at the time allowed you to copy and even overcome the situation around you."

Rozner then digs deep into emotional Intelligence and leadership, highlighting how these emotional competencies can revolutionize your PM career. This chapter brightens up memories we usually shy away from, reminding you that you're in good company. Grab Mark's toolkit, face your fears with a smile, and step into a brighter, better you!

I'm proud to associate with this book because it has added to my skill set and can do the same for you. If you enjoy it, share it. Spread the word, help others to make a difference in the world by applying these next-level project management skills.

Terry Dean Schmidt, author of
Strategic Project Management Made Simple

Introduction

At the heart of this book's purpose is the conviction that there is a fast-approaching problem in the workforce at large and in project management specifically: the risk of lost knowledge due to retirement. It's no secret that the "Baby Boomer" generation is rapidly reaching retirement age.[1]

It doesn't take deep investigation to recognize the large risks of lost knowledge as a large section of the workforce exits due to retirement. Project management is not immune to this oncoming issue. According to the Project Management Institute (PMI), "[b]y 2030, just 77 million project management employees out of the current workforce will be left due to re-

---

1   U.S. Census Bureau (2019). *2020 Census Will Help Policymakers Prepare for the Incoming Wave of Aging Boomers.* https://www.census.gov/library/stories/2019/12/by-2030-all-baby-boomers-will-be-age-65-or-older.html, accessed 8/13/2023.

tirement.[2]

As of this writing in 2023, PMI estimates there are 90 million project management-oriented employees currently in projectized industries across the world, and 1.2 million holders of Project Management Professional (PMP) certification worldwide.[3]

What does this mean for the future of project management? As 2030 approaches, not only will a great number of project jobs will open due to new positions being created, but millions of roles will open due to retirement.[4]

With projected demand for more than 2.3 million new project managers per year and only 1.2 million PMI certified project management professionals globally in total, the worrisome math begins to paint a picture in which supply becomes overwhelmed by demand in the near future.

The core thesis behind this book is that proactive, deliberate communication is the solution to mitigate the effects of lost knowledge in the project management field. While the resources provided by PMI are impressive and helpful for many project managers, placing the burden of communicating everything on one institution is doomed to fail.

Rather, project management will be well-served by individuals coming together to create collaborative communities of practice to communicate and learn from one another. The experience of established project managers should be prized for its value just as much as the eagerness to learn of project managers early in their careers. If project managers can cultivate vibrant environments where learning and knowledge

---

[2] PMI (2021). *Talent Gap: Ten-Year Employment Trends, Costs, and Global Implications.* https://www.pmi.org/learning/careers/talent-gap-2021, accessed 8/13/2023.

[3] PMI (2023). *Project Management Professional (PMP)®.* https://www.pmi.org/certifications/project-management-pmp, accessed 8/13/2023.

[4] PMI (2023). *Global Project Management Job Trends 2023.* https://www.pmi.org/learning/careers/global-job-trends-2023, accessed 8/13/2023.

sharing are prioritized, the field of project management will grow buffers against lost knowledge.

Most project managers will be familiar with the concept of "Lessons Learned," a feature prominent in the closing process group outlined in PMI's framework for predictive project management. Lessons gleaned from throughout the lifecycle of the project should be gathered, discussed, communicated to relevant stakeholders, and archived in a repository for reference in preparation and planning of future projects.

Regardless of how we regard the formal definition of the Lessons Learned framework, the idea of focusing time and effort on communicating experienced knowledge is a valuable one. While nothing can replace direct, in-person communication and active observations while projects are being executed, this book can be considered an attempt to communicate project management lessons from a variety of industries, experience levels, and perspectives.

This book includes essays with a focus on how project managers earlier in their careers can guide projects effectively while also generating career opportunities for themselves. Readers will find insights based on real-work experience that transcend theories that may not translate in a practical way. Our goal is to provide advice and ideas that may prove helpful now and in future years as project management continues to develop as we near 2030.

This book is the product of a confluence of factors: good fortune, strong community, and the recognition of the knowledge gap that will widen in the coming years. Throughout 2022, a group of people working in project management began to form on social media, leading to a vibrant exchange of ideas and new initiatives. As this community grew and developed, it became apparent that we were enriched by the diversity of experience and expertise in it.

A theme of this community was the exchange of information between new project managers transitioning to the field from other disciplines or functions. A significant number of questions arose from new members looking for guidance on navigating projects, finding career opportunities, and gaining knowledge beyond a certification framework. As our group grew, the gaps in knowledge became more apparent and the need for reliable guidance became pressing.

The idea for this book was developed by several members of this online project management community on LinkedIn. As time went on, it became clear that the project would benefit by a pivot to incorporating many voices. It was a natural idea to bring this community of thinkers together to contribute their expertise to others entering the project management field.

The authors of this book have a wealth of experience in a wide variety of project-related roles. Some have experience in large construction or engineering projects. Others come from a background in software or other fields that are not considered "typical" for project management. Some of our authors have worked in program management and others for PMOs. The fact is that projects come in all shapes and sizes and pervade many industries where the projects are executed without the label "project management" ever being applied to the endeavors that deliver valuable deliverables.

Our goal in bringing together this group of professionals is to impart lessons and ideas, born from experience, that transcend the specifics on a single project. The distillation of knowledge from managing many projects over the course of years can serve as a powerful tool for project managers looking for help making the most out of their career delivering value to their organizations.

In the end, we wish that our readers will derive value from the lessons included in this book and pass that knowledge on to others learning and growing in the project management field. We are all part of a worldwide community, and we are grateful for your contributions to retaining and building upon the lessons we have learned throughout our careers.

There are simply too many lessons to be communicated in a book this way. The collective experience and wisdom of the individuals who have contributed to this work could likely fill several hefty bookshelves, if not its own considerable library.

Despite its limitations, we believe that this book will provide insightful guidance for project managers looking for down-to-earth guidance on what it takes to be a successful project manager.

A final additional goal for this collection is to continue the growth and development of an organic project management community to share knowledge and ideas. This invaluable work will facilitate the exchange of concepts and techniques in all directions, across multiple generations of project managers. It is our hope that the readers of this book will reach out and connect with the professionals who contributed to this book and continue the conversation that is so critical to the relevance and effectiveness of our field.

Executing Excellence

CHAPTER ONE

Solving the Paradox of Project Success

By Adrian Dooley

I have been involved in project, program and portfolio management (P3M) for over 45 years, in many different roles. It has provided me with a worthwhile and enjoyable career but has not been without its frustrations. I see so many organizations fail to achieve the benefits of good P3M for reasons that can and should be addressed.

In this essay I suggest some of the reasons why this situation has arisen and how they may be addressed. At the end, I will explain how this is not just a theory and we have a community that has already provided many practical solutions.

Introduction

Some projects succeed, some projects fail. 'Twas ever thus and always will be.

Naturally, we are rather more obsessed with the ones that fail. Perhaps because failure costs us money; perhaps because we aren't getting the benefits we had expected; perhaps simply because we are project professionals, and we strive to do better.

Nearly 30 years ago, Martin Cobb, the then CIO for the Treasury Board of Canada, uttered the words that became known as Cobb's Paradox:

> "We know why projects fail; we know how to prevent their failure – so why do they still fail?"

Academics would argue that this is not a true paradox so in this essay, I will take what Martin Cobb said as a hypothesis and break it into three parts. I'll look at the evidence that suggests we know why projects fail, the evidence that we know how to stop them failing and then suggest why they still fail.

Before I start, two quick notes on terminology.

Firstly, we have become used to talking about projects, programs and portfolios as if they are three separate and mutually exclusive types of initiative. This is not the case. They are actually points on a continuum. While there are initiatives that are conveniently classed as projects and others that are conveniently classed as programs, there are many initiatives that demonstrate the characteristics of both – in graduated degrees. In this essay, I want to cover the whole continuum.

Project Delivery is a useful collective term for project, program and portfolio management. It's more natural and elegant than abbreviations like P3M. I can't claim the credit for this term as it was fairly recently coined by the UK Government's latest standard (GovS002). You might ask what authority has the UK Government in this? I would simply answer that if it wasn't for UK Government guidance published in the 1990s, we wouldn't be talking about projects, programs and portfolios, as separate entities, in the way we do now. We're coming full circle.

Secondly, another popular term is 'Best Practice'. Project delivery is a hugely diverse discipline. It covers all industries and professions; it includes simple, complicated and complex initiatives. There is no one, single 'best' way of managing this diversity. We can adapt 'generally accepted good practice' to specific contexts and may argue that this leads to best practices in localised, well-defined contexts – but there is no such thing as generic project delivery best practice.

Therefore, in this essay, I will talk about good practice in project delivery.

Part 1: "We know why projects fail…"

We all know success when we see it and we all know failure when we see it. But does the person next to you view the results of project delivery in exactly the same way? Perceptions of project delivery success and failure are actually quite subjective but that is not the way they are usually presented.

Next time you see something that says "70 percent of projects fail", bear in mind that this was probably a survey of self-selecting respondents from a particular subset of the profession (e.g., clients of a particular consultancy who focus on specific types of IT) using a narrow, objective definition of success or failure. Then walk out into a world where so many infrastructure and IT projects make it possible for you to go about your day-to-day business – successfully. I think it is reasonable to believe that there are a lot of people out there who know how to make projects succeed. It's not all doom and gloom.

If you follow the profession closely, you will inevitably see the results of numerous surveys that try to determine what is going wrong in projects that do fail. They crop up on social media all the time, and in the days before social media they were a staple of magazine articles and consultancy brochures.

The earliest example I saw of just such a survey was from 1972. It was presented at a meeting of the IPMA (International Project Management Association). Rarely a week goes by that I don't see another survey of reasons why projects fail – mainly on LinkedIn. They typically include lists of 'reasons' such as:

- Unclear objectives.
- Ill-considered changes.
- Lack of communication.
- Lack of end user input.
- Insufficient or excessive control.

What is very noticeable is that the latest lists look pretty much the same as the one from over 50 years ago (and all the ones in-between). The same 'reasons' keep coming up time and time again, decade after decade. This would support the implicit suggestion in Cobb's Paradox that nothing is changing. Projects continue to fail for the same old "reasons."

You may wonder why, in these last couple of paragraphs, that I put the word "reasons" in quotation marks. It is because I firmly believe they are not reasons, in reality they are symptoms. These symptoms are what you see when a project fails but they are not the root causes.

Does that mean we don't know why projects fail?
It depends.
If you talk to someone who is only aware of these lists, then they will quote them as reasons why projects fail. It could be argued that this person, through no real fault of their own,

does not truly understand the root causes of failure.

More experienced project professionals know that there are other underlying issues that need to be addressed. I'll come to these later, but first let's have a look at some more evidence relating to failure.

Over my career, I became aware of plenty of anecdotal evidence that people were not adequately applying the project management basics. I frequently came across situations where people were floundering, or their project was in deep trouble, for completely avoidable reasons.

In the last few years, I have been able to obtain texts of lessons learned reports from many different organizations. I'll just pick a few of the more obviously basic issues that project teams only realized once their projects were underway or even finished:

"Ensure the project has adequate financial commitment to fully deliver the required outcomes."

"Fully consider the pros and cons of the chosen procurement route before proceeding."

"Involve business stakeholders from the start."

"Overoptimistic schedules can lead to poor behaviours. Significant costs are time-based so it is important to get the schedule right."

"Clearly identify priority and reason for project (It changes depending on who you ask)."

"Initial baseline measurements of areas in which benefit is to be claimed must be in place at least before implementation."

"Existing benefit management documentation is not fully current and actual measurements have not been recorded."
..and probably my favourite:

"Having a formal business case would have been beneficial."

Wow! Who'd have thought that knowing why we started this project and what we wanted to achieve would have been useful?

To me, this illustrates where the lists of symptoms come from. They are what we did wrong, not why we did it wrong.

So, considering the first part of Cobb's Paradox, do we know why projects fail? My conclusion is "Yes, we do have the implicit knowledge, but we are not good at making that explicit". Projects do not fail for the reasons we are regularly fed but for things more fundamental. This superficial presentation of failure causes problems when we get to the second phrase.

Part 2: "...we know how to prevent their failure..."

The world of project delivery is well served with good practice guidance made up of standards, bodies of knowledge, methodologies and a host of other publications. Some of these are books written by a single author and some (typically those produced by professional bodies) have thousands of contributors.

While all these guides look very different, any sort of detailed comparison reveals that they say pretty much the same things – they're just packaged differently.

Given the thousands of people involved in developing this

good practice, there would have to be monumental groupthink for it to be fundamentally wrong. Of course, there are different perspectives and different solutions, but projects are incredibly diverse and there is room for many different adaptations.

Let's go back to the "reasons why projects fail" and the "lessons learned" for a moment.

What good practice guidance does not start by emphasising the need for clear objectives, what guidance does not recommend communicating with stakeholders from the very start and what guidance does not stress the importance of a business case?

Every year, tens of thousands of people are trained in this good practice. These people go on to manage projects and I'm sure many succeed (more than the surveys would have us believe) but many do not.

When all this good guidance is out there, why do so many people not realize that the basics work until it's too late?

Perhaps, as the author Douglas Adams so wittily observed:

"Human beings, who are almost unique in having the ability to learn from the experience of others, are also remarkable for their apparent disinclination to do so."

On the whole, I would agree that we know how to prevent a lot of failure. I also suggest that the problem is not that everyone needs PhD level knowledge of project delivery, it's that the basics are not well applied.

We need to get past the symptoms and dig out the root causes.

Part 3: "...so why do they still fail?"

In my opinion there are many factors that stop the fundamentals being applied effectively. Some are more significant than others, but they all add up to a series of barriers that need to be broken down. I don't have an exhaustive list because we identify new barriers all the time, but here are the ones I've identified so far:

- Good practice content.
- Integration of different categories of guidance.
- Accessibility and relevance.
- Embedding good practice in day-to-day activity.
- 'Monday morning.'
- Long-term personal development.
- Diverse teams.
- Organizational maturity.

Integration of Different Categories of Guidance

Good practice guidance generally comes in five flavours: Knowledge, Method, Competence, Maturity and Techniques and Models.

Knowledge comprises the functions that make up the discipline of project delivery. Topics like scope management, risk management, stakeholder management and so on.

Method comprises the processes that provide a framework for using the functions. This is typically based on a lifecycle and explains who does what and when, in different phases of the lifecycle.

Competence describes the knowledge of functions and processes that an individual needs, and the performance criteria that should meet, in order to perform their role competently.
Maturity describes the attributes that must be achieved across an organization in order to reach levels of Capability Maturity (typically from 1 to 5) that indicate how well project delivery is performed.

Techniques and Models are the detailed elements that are needed to perform the functions and processes. They comprise techniques such as Qualitative Risk Analysis, Critical Chain or Scrum, and models of personal interactions such as Hersey and Blanchard on leadership or Thomas-Killman on conflict management.

The historical problem here is that individual guides focus on one of these areas and if they address two, it is never comprehensive. It is widely recognized that an effective project delivery organization must apply a framework that covers all five areas.

The status quo leads to two typical problems.

Firstly, there are those organizations that think they can survive on just one form of published guidance: "We have applied the XXX methodology so our project delivery will be fine," completely forgetting about applying the functions, having competent people and developing organizational maturity.

Secondly, there are organizations that recognize the need for all five areas and realize that they need to adapt five different publications that have different taxonomies and use different terminology. They embark on trying to harmonise five different guides which often turns out to be too hard, take too long or cost too much – and it becomes a failed project in its own right.

Solution Number 1: we need an integrated framework that covers all five areas with a single taxonomy and consistent terminology.

Accessibility and Relevance

Let's assume that someone is going to take a market leading example from each of the five areas and harmonised them. They would have an expensive pile of publications of significant length when placed end-to-end.

Of course, generic guidance needs to be tailored to the specific context of an organization in order to be relevant. The last thing you want is for individuals involved in project delivery to be encumbered with irrelevant functions or inappropriate processes.

So you embark on harmonising the five chosen guides, trying to engineer them into well-fitting jigsaw pieces, only to find that much of what you want to use is subject to copyright. So perhaps you provide a "guide to the guides." "In our context, use that bit of that guide and that bit of that guide, with this adaptation."

No one running a project or program has time to trawl through all this documentation, even if you were prepared to pay the price of having a copy for every team member.

And of course, good practice is not static. It evolves continuously but published guides are typically updated only every five or six years.

Solution Number 2: Good practice needs to be freely available, simply navigated, easily tailorable and regularly updated.

"Monday Morning"

While the title might be a little obscure, I find that a lot of people identify with this problem that I would like initially to illustrate with a brief true story.

In the mid-1980s I ran a lot of training courses on a project scheduling package called SuperProject. On one occasion as the delegates entered the room for a new course, I thought I recognized a familiar face.

"Hello," I said offering my hand, "I'm sure we've met before but I'm sorry, I can't remember where and when."

His smile was warm but slightly sheepish. "Yes," he said "I was on one of your courses six weeks ago but I never got the chance to apply what I learned and by now I've forgotten most of it. So here I am again."

This would be a situation well recognized by the 19th Century German psychologist, Hermann Ebbinghaus, who documented this effect in his eponymous 'Forgetting Curve.' Ebbinghaus suggested that without repetition and application, after a month you are likely to only retain about 20 percent of information you have learnt.

We can couple this with the 70:20:10 model of McCall, Lombardo and Eichinger from the 1980s. This suggests that only 10 percent of knowledge comes from 'structured education – off the job' (this is due in large part, I would suggest, to Ebbinghaus's curve), while 20 percent comes from 'social learning – near the job' and 70 percent comes from 'experiential learning – on the job.'

My poor delegate who had to attend the course a second

time, could have been saved the time and expense if only his organization had given him the opportunity to apply what he had learned immediately after the first course.

That's why I call this barrier "Monday morning." Tens of thousands of people attend basic project delivery training every year. This often takes one week, and they may even take an exam on Friday to show that they have retained a lot of knowledge. They then go home for a relaxing weekend and on Monday morning go back to a week's backlog of work in the office and...

...carry on doing things the way they always did.

Solution Number 3: People need to be given the opportunity and supporting tools that help them apply new knowledge in the workplace, especially after intensive courses where their minds have been crammed with a lot of new information.

Long-Term Personal Development

The current trend for certification in project delivery started in the 1980s and its popularity continues unabated. This popularity is a double-edged sword. On the positive side, it promotes the idea that you need to be knowledgeable to run projects and rewards people for gaining that knowledge.

The downside is that what different certifications say about their holders is regularly over-inflated and treated as an end in itself, as opposed to a milestone on a journey of professional development.

Too many people and companies believe that a one-week course and exam makes someone a competent project delivery manager. That is patently not the case.

Solution Number 4: Certifications need to be seen as milestones on a journey that starts with basic knowledge and progresses to competence in managing increasingly complex projects and programs.

Diverse Teams

Projects and programs are delivered by people and those people do not all see the world in the same way. All the members of a team may go on the same training course and learn the same good practice but then interpret and apply it in very different ways.

These different approaches are neither right nor wrong, they are simply alternative interpretations. Problems arise when people believe their expectations of how good practice should be applied are the "one true way" and don't understand that others see things differently.

There are often unspoken differences in opinion about how effectively work is being managed and assumptions based on personal interpretations can result in conflict between managers, sponsors, stakeholders, and team members.

Underlying differences can often stay beneath the surface until it's too late to deal with the consequences.

Solution Number 5: Good practice needs to accommodate different personality-based interpretations and organizations need to foster approaches that enable people to understand those differences, identify their effects and act upon the results.

Organizational Maturity

The concept of organizational Capability Maturity was first developed by Carnegie Mellon University in 1987. It was developed as a framework for improving processes and performance across various domains. An organization's maturity level in project delivery is an indicator of how consistently it will deliver successful projects and programs.

The important point here is that a Capability Maturity based approach recognizes the diverse factors that lead to successful project delivery. It's not just about training people or documented good practice or developing competent individuals. It's about all of these and more.

An organization that seeks to improve its Capability Maturity is one that recognizes the need to take a holistic approach to breaking down the barriers to embedding good practice and improving project delivery. A mature organization is one that has broken down those barriers and is reaping the rewards.

Solution Number 6: Commit organizationally to all aspects of embedding good practice and measure progress towards achieving a mature organization.

A Solution?

It's easy to talk in theoretical terms about the barriers to embedding project delivery good practice. It's more difficult to come up with ideas for solutions and even harder to apply them. I started this essay by saying that I had had a worthwhile and enjoyable 45-year career in project delivery (so far).

As the conclusion of this career, I have led the development of something called the Praxis Framework, which is designed to overcome the barriers I have highlighted. This has helped many people and organizations already and I hope it will continue to help individuals, teams, and organizations improve their project delivery long after I have finally retired.

Solution Number 1: We need an integrated framework that covers all five areas with a single taxonomy and consistent terminology. The Praxis Framework integrates all five areas with a single taxonomy and consistent terminology.

Solution Number 2: Good practice needs to be freely available, simply navigated, easily tailorable and regularly updated. The Framework is freely available at www.praxisframework.org, a sort of Wikipedia for project delivery. It is community-driven, with frequent updates and provides tools (like Praxis Local) that demonstrate how it can be tailored and made even more accessible.

Solution Number 3: People need to be given the opportunity and supporting tools that help them apply new knowledge in the workplace, especially after intensive courses where their minds have been crammed with a lot of new information.

Praxis contains a free tool called Praxis 360, inspired by Atul Gawande's book *The Checklist Manifesto,* which tells the story of how he developed checklists that resulted in surgical mortality around the world being reduced by 40 percent.

Praxis 360 is made up of a series of checklists for each function and process in the framework. By working through the checklists soon after any form of training, individuals start to apply what they have learned. By doing so they take the 10 percent of learning into the 20 percent and 70 percent realms and start to embed effective habits.

Solution Number 4: Certifications need to be seen as milestones on a journey that starts with basic knowledge and progresses to competence in managing increasingly complex projects and programs.

Praxis offers certifications but promotes the idea that a short knowledge-based courses alone do not make a competent project or program manager. The development path goes all the way from basic knowledge to assessment of competence in complex environments. Tools like Praxis 360 and Team Praxis (see next section) are there to help people along that path.

Solution Number 5: Good practice needs to accommodate different personality-based interpretations and organizations need to foster approaches that enable people to understand those differences, identify their effects and act upon the results.

One of the most common models for personality assessment is William Marston's DISC model. Team Praxis uses this to explore different interpretations on a topic-by-topic basis. It helps individuals communicate better and the team to play to its individual strengths.

In conjunction with Team Praxis, using Praxis 360 to gather and collate multiple views of how projects and programs are being managed, develops a common understanding and highlights differences early on, while there is still time to act upon them.

Solution Number 6: Commit organizationally to all aspects of embedding good practice and measure progress towards achieving a mature organization.

The biggest hurdle to this commitment is the perceived time and cost. A conventional approach of "first assessment – improvement program – second assessment," can take anything from one to three years.

But if you are already working on embedding good practice this can happen iteratively and incrementally much more efficiently. The checklists in Praxis 360 serve a third purpose because they are based on CMMI attributes. If they are used to help individuals apply their knowledge and develop competency, and by teams to identify areas of agreement and differences, they automatically develop organizational maturity.

Praxis 360 even provides a real time dashboard of increasing maturity and highlights areas that need improvement.

What Does the Future Hold?

It would be arrogant in the extreme to suggest that I have identified all the barriers and all the solutions. We constantly search for more.

As I sit here, writing these words, the weight of topical discussion in the world of project delivery is moving from Agile to Artificial Intelligence. Everyone who wants more "likes" on social media is telling us what AI can do for us and giving us lists of prompts we should be using for ChatGPT.

I have no idea how AI really works but I can see its enormous potential – with one major reservation. When I ask Chat GPT about something I don't know much about, it comes back with highly eloquent and very convincing answers – it's wonderful. When I ask Chat GPT about project delivery, it often comes back with eloquent and convincing garbage – it's terrible.

The problem is that LLMs are trained on all the information on the web and have no ability to distinguish what is good information from what is uninformed clickbait.

I have seen articles posted by highly reputable news organizations that completely misrepresent the way projects are managed. A bit of investigation shows that the 'authors' of these articles have no background in project delivery at all and the articles themselves have all the hallmarks of having been written by AI.

I am reliably informed that search engines and LLMs give information from 'trusted' sources greater credibility when providing new responses and writing new articles. So having given misleading information to non-expert journalists, who then publish it primarily as a vehicle for selling advertising, that misinformation is amplified and institutionalised. I'm sure this problem exists in so many areas – but I am only qualified to talk about it in my own area of expertise.

AI should be another means of breaking down the barriers to embedding good practice. It should be there at your side, reminding you that a solid business case with clear objectives will increase the likelihood of your project's success, and perhaps even helping you write that very business case. What it shouldn't be doing is telling you that Scrum is a project management methodology, or that 'Planning' is a project life cycle phase.

I believe what is needed is LLM trained on credible, authoritative good practice and a group of us are working on just such a tool. Who knows, by the time this essay is published, we might even have it working.

Summary

I believe Cobb's Paradox is true. I think we do know why projects fail and we do know how to make fewer of them fail, but we simply don't do it for a host of reasons.

We need to do what every good sportsperson does – practice the basics and get them right. The boring stuff! If you make those basics a habit, then you can start to think about doing the clever (and much more interesting) stuff. Like every successful sportsperson, you can never stop practicing the basics if you want to keep delivering the clever stuff. Failure happens when you lose that foundation.

I hope this essay has given you a few insights into the root causes of this problem and ideas for what you might do about it, assuming of course that all your projects don't succeed already.

Note: It's only been a couple of months since I wrote this essay and said what I thought the future holds. Oh, how the world has moved on since then. We now have a dedicated AI bot for project management called Marvin.

We only feed Marvin on content from credible sources and the initial reaction has been very positive. Many people support our idea of AI as a public service and have donated excellent IP that is not available on the internet. We add more every week.

I'd tell you about its capabilities but by the time you read this it would be out of date. To keep abreast of developments, please connect with me on LinkedIn where I regularly post about developments.

CHAPTER TWO

Freelancing and Project Management

By Kayla McGuire

The last few years have given rise to the freelancer and one-person business, and this trend isn't going away anytime soon. Fueled by a desire for more freedom of time along with an interest in building multiple revenue streams for financial security, people all over the world are leveraging their experience to create opportunities for themselves outside of traditional employment. And project managers are no exception.

Maybe you are thinking: "Freelancing as a project manager? Does it really make sense?"

You bet it does. And here's why: projects are, by nature, temporary endeavors with a unique purpose. They don't go on forever. This means the people who manage projects have positions that are essentially governed by these temporary endeavors. Companies, particularly those operating lean or heavily projectized, have increasingly begun to hire temporary workers to help manage projects, understanding that full-time employment doesn't always make sense for project work. The result is as Dice reported in May 2023:

> "There are over 128,000 open freelance project manager jobs in the United States alone."

The truly fascinating part of this phenomenon is that whether you seek long-term contract positions with established companies, flexible freelance or "gig" jobs with smaller teams, or have your eyes on launching a full on consultancy service, there is room for you in this market.

For the remainder of this article I will refer to the independent project manager as a freelancer, meant to encompass all genres of independent project management work.

As a freelance project manager turned business consultant, I've seen my share of projects and clients. One of the more interesting aspects of my journey has been the diversity of my own work. I've grown from managing a few projects here and there, to partnering with CEOs to build and execute programs, to providing strategic consulting to entrepreneurs who are launching new initiatives.

My work has spanned industries and given me a full circle glimpse into the depth of project management and what is possible within this discipline. I hope my own journey gives you hope that you absolutely can land the ideal type of work for you in a freelance market. All it takes is a vision, strategy, and consistent effort. The good news is, you're not alone. I'm here to help.

First Things First

If we were in a coaching session together, one of the first questions I might ask is, "what kind of project manager do you want to be?" This is because it is important for you to set goals that are in alignment with your self-identified purpose. It is only by taking the time to understand what you want out of your life and career that you will ever achieve success. The answer to this question will guide you in your approach to landing the right work and further managing your career.

To aid in this exercise, I invite you to take a moment to write down your personal vision statement. Consider the type of project manager you want to be to your leadership team, co-workers, and clients. Consider the behaviors, attitudes, and values that you want to demonstrate. Consider how you want to treat yourself and be treated. Once you have this figured out, start acting like this person *today*. This is the first step.

In the pages that follow I offer three important skill areas to focus on as you consider launching your freelance project management work. These skills are not meant to be a replacement for good old fashioned project management, but rather as a complement to help you achieve your highest potential as a freelance project manager.

Skill Number 1: Get Comfortable with Navigating the Unknown

Get used to ambiguity, because for the freelancer this is your new normal. The work you do as a freelancer often requires a different set of skills than that of the typical 9-5 employee. You are part investigator and part implementer. You are part operational strategist and part client liaison. And in your personal business, you are part salesperson and part accountant. Of course, the exact work that you do will depend on the type of company, industry, and more. However, with typical freelance gigs there won't be a handbook waiting in your inbox on your first day, and you definitely won't have a manager standing by to tell you exactly how it's done. Instead, your clients will be looking to *you* to tell *them* how to do it.

This means that no matter how adept you are with project management theory, you will need to feel confident in your ability to evaluate a situation and provide smart recommendations for your clients. You will need to understand how to practice effective project management in a variety of scenarios.

As such, more successful freelancers often have significant background and experience in project management (whether through official positions with the "Project Manager" title, or via project-centered adjacent roles).

In general, it is recommended to secure several years of real-world experience in your niche prior to diving off into a full-time freelance career, although there are no hard and fast rules.

I never knew just how uncomfortable I was with ambiguity until I was thrown into it head first. When I landed as a project manager with a fast-moving tech startup in 2019, I had over six years of technical project management experience, and additionally had built and operated a business of my own for several years. I thought I had seen it all, but boy was I wrong!

I vividly remember coming home after that first day of work. I had learned the project board was a mess and the team was frustrated, misaligned, and confused. It was my job to fix it and I didn't know where to start! With no handbook or SOP to follow, I began to carve a path by combining my experience with my project management training and my own intuition.

Over the weeks that followed I worked with the team to define goals, align teams, break down work, and start tackling tasks in sprints to achieve goals. We began to operate like a team instead of individual contributors working on different things. And while we weren't able to pull the whole thing around (the doors closed in early 2020 due to lack of funding), I did learn a lot about how to effectively operate in organizations with heightened ambiguity.

This experience now stands out as the catalyst to my pursuit of project management as both a career AND a passion. It is what sparked my interest in educating and supporting project managers through my YouTube channel and resulted in the formation of my consulting business.

I've since been in a variety of "ambiguous" workplaces, and now feel comfortable working through the confusion and noise to distill work into simple next steps. This confidence is what is needed in order to thrive as a freelance project manager.

Pro Tip: Work with Startups to Gain Experience

An excellent way to gain hands-on experience with navigating the unknown is by working with small businesses and startup companies. This is a particularly excellent option for early career professionals interested in starting a business themselves one day.

Startups offer a crash course in real world business with the potential to influence every aspect of the organization. These organizations often don't have the budget for a full-time project manager, but desperately need help wrangling resources to meet deadlines. Working with these teams in a fractional or freelance capacity can be a real win-win situation.

While landing contracts with startups and small companies is a smart strategy for freelancers to secure business, it's important to understand that working with these organizations is very different from being employed by an established enterprise. In the absence of process and bureaucracy, there is heightened ambiguity which may feel chaotic to some freelancers. This is usually because small teams are figuring it all out for the first time, alongside a strict budget, hefty investor demands, junior staff, and a tight timeline. Project managers who need structure and order should proceed with this awareness.

Ten Tips for Navigating the Unknown

In my coaching and consulting work, I often speak with project managers who are in particularly tricky situations. Some are leading big initiatives for the first time and others are leading efforts to operationalize new business units or even entire organizations. The following tips have provided them support and guidance as they navigate the unknown, and I offer them to you as well.

1. Listen, ask questions, and take notes religiously.

2. Communicate with your team early and often.

3. Understand that no one has all of the answers, you are all working through it together.

4. Never lose sight of the vision, and make sure everyone agrees on what that is.

5. Continually evaluate your plan. Check out the book "Lean Business Planning" by Tim Berry for help.

6. Work on your mindset. As Adam Grant once said, reframe "I don't know what I'm doing" to "I don't know what I'm doing yet."

7. Trust your gut, often the simple answer is the best solution, and if you don't know where to start, ask questions until it becomes clear to you.

Learn how to tell the difference between value-add activities and time-wasters. Often productivity becomes about doing less in order to do more.

1. Make data-informed decisions as much as possible, especially when it comes to pivoting.

2. Don't take things personally.

Skill Number 2: Networking and Building a Solid Reputation

It's no secret that networking is one of the keys to building a successful career. As a traditional 9-5 employee, building a solid foundation of colleagues is invaluable. But as a freelancer, you will soon discover that your network is truly the lifeblood of your work. The importance of building and maintaining a solid network cannot be stressed enough, and efforts to cultivate a network should be ongoing in the life of a freelancer.

When I first began my freelancing journey, my "network" consisted of a short list of former colleagues and stale LinkedIn connections. I had never attended an in-person networking event, never publicly created content, and my idea of "staying in touch" was waving at acquaintances when I saw them every three years at the grocery store.

So when it came time to search for freelancing work, I started where so many well-meaning freelancers do – online job boards and freelance marketplaces. I spent hundreds of hours creating profiles, applying for work, and submitting bids for random jobs, mostly to no avail. It just wasn't working.

It wasn't until a distant connection unexpectedly reached out to ask what I was up to that I realized my network was larger than I thought. In fact, it never would have never occurred to me to reach out to this particular person who had been a trusted vendor partner at a previous workplace.

As it turns out, when this connection learned about my freelance status they expressed genuine interest in working with me. This interest was due to the mutual positive experience we had experienced years prior. The conversation resulted in my securing a three-month contract with his company, thus providing inspiration to further tap into and build out my network.

I now focus time each day to grow my network and cultivate relationships with existing connections. And let me tell you, it pays off: the vast majority of the revenue for my business comes from my network.

If you want to make sure you never have to go through the dreaded "job search" as a freelancer or otherwise, I highly suggest you invest time regularly to grow your network.

Five Tips to Build Your Network

1. Reach out to colleagues and friends to learn about their needs and share your freelancing status. Be natural and conversational - don't worry about overtly "selling."

2. Start a LinkedIn creator account to begin sharing your expertise and make new connections.

3. Attend in-person business networking events in your area.

4. Join your local PMI chapter or other relevant professional groups.

5. Create a schedule to follow-up and check-in regularly with key contacts in order to maintain relationships.

Pro Tip: It's Natural to Be Hesitant to Reach Out, but Do It Anyway

Most people I speak with express concern about reaching out to their network or posting content online. They worry they will be judged or, in some cases, they are concerned about job security (if they are currently employed).

Certainly, you will want to proceed with caution in situations where your current employer may frown upon your freelance activity.

On the other hand, if your hesitation stems from simple discomfort about putting yourself out there, rest assured this is normal and we have all been there. When I began my LinkedIn content creation journey I had a measly 500 connections and questioned whether I belonged on the platform at all!

Now, however, thousands and thousands of connections later, I can confidently say the beginning discomfort was absolutely worth it. I've built relationships, invited connections to work on paid collaborations with me, and traveled across the US to deliver projects. And this is all due to pushing a little button that says "post." Trust me, try pushing past the discomfort and see what happens.

In fact, you may be surprised by how many folks from your past are excited to hear about your new status as a freelancer. The most common response I've received is "I'm so jealous! I wish I could do that! Could you share your strategy?"

Some of these folks have even developed into coaching clients or attended my freelance project manager bootcamps. I share this with you to offer encouragement and as a reminder that people generally want others to succeed. Assuming the best is always the way to go.

Seven Tips to Stand Out and Build a Solid Reputation in Your Freelancing Work

Along with building your network, it's important to ensure your reputation is rock solid. This will not only strengthen your existing relationships but can open the door to new business and really help you stand out as a key person to know in your area of expertise.

1. Go the extra mile to learn about the organization, project, and subject matter.

2. Check in with your team regularly and ask them how they are doing.

3. Get to know people you work with on an appropriately personal level. Ask questions!

4. Offer help or support when appropriate.

5. Always do what you say you are going to do.

6. Show you actually care by listening, recalling details, and following up.

7. Set firm expectations and uphold your boundaries. Self-respect is powerful.

Skill Number 3: Communicating Your Value

As a freelancer, being able to communicate your value and the results you produce are critical. Freelancers will find themselves struggling to attract and maintain clients if they cannot communicate exactly why prospects should hire them (value) and how their work has contributed to goals (results).

Whether you are speaking to a recruiter, hiring manager, C-suite executive, or entrepreneur you need to be able to clearly and concisely tell them who you are, what you do, and why you're worth the investment. Additionally, learning to tell your story in an impactful way is worth its weight in gold.

Communicating Value

One of the biggest roadblocks to landing work is not being able to effectively communicate your value. Often contributing to this issue is when a freelance project manager simply advertises as a "freelance project manager." The reason why this is a problem is because the term "project manager" can mean different things to different people and can vary industry to industry.

Before introducing yourself simply as a "freelance project manager," I suggest considering what project management means to you, where you excel, and what you have to offer.

This discovery is particularly important in the world of project management as the rabbit hole can be deep. Do you want to focus on project leadership or stakeholder management or meeting facilitation? Do you want to specialize in a certain software tool or methodology? Do you want to serve as a project management trainer or actually manage projects yourself?

You may want to revisit the exercise you completed at the beginning of this chapter, further exploring your own personal vision and the type of project manager you want to be. This introspection will help you home in on your true value.

When I began my freelancing journey, I knew I wanted to zero in on startups, my area of expertise. Not only did I love this work and have extensive experience in it, but I also recognized there was a real lack of support for project managers in startup organizations. This focus gave me material and inspiration to launch my YouTube channel which, at the time, was solely focused on startup project management.

However, as time has progressed, I've adjusted my niche and services to respond to what the market wants. My focus has shifted from "how to manage projects at startups" to "how to become a freelance project manager" and even "how to launch your own business."

I've learned that I can spin my wheels forever on what I want to do, but if it doesn't align with what the market needs then I will never make money on it. Instead of focusing on what I want to do, I keep the focus on my clients, audience, and broader market by continually asking "What do they want? What do they need? What will they pay for?"

The best way to learn what people need and will pay for is by asking questions and observing their behavior. This will allow you to identify the sweet spot of where your passion and expertise align with what the market needs and will pay for. A great resource to check out on this topic is the Japanese concept called "ikigai."

Sorting this out is only the beginning. Now you need to land business, and the only way to do that is by showing that you are worth the investment, just like in a traditional job search.

Seven Tips to Communicate Your Value

1. Speak the language of your prospect.
2. Develop an elevator pitch to clearly describe who you are, relevant background, and achievements in 30 seconds or less.
3. Know your pricing and their budget.
4. Clearly lay out your approach and how you will deliver results. Do you use a framework or methodology or system?
5. Provide social proof in the form of references, LinkedIn recommendations, or verified testimonials.
6. Share a portfolio of your work: case studies, white papers, etc.
7. Be prepared to focus on sharing the **results** of your work.

Pro Tip: Build a Portfolio to Showcase Your Successful Results

Set yourself up for successful results by establishing clear expectations at the start of any job. Ensure alignment about goals, priorities, and authority. Gather baseline metrics or data points and compile into weekly reporting to track progress.

Write a "before" profile at the start of your project capturing current state and desired future state for use in a case study. Take notes and retrospect weekly, documenting any significant improvements, insights, or setbacks.

Write case studies, create infographics, and use other creative methods to document your impact after project completion. Finally, gather testimonials from clients and team members and creatively use them in your portfolio, LinkedIn profile, resume, website, etc.

Conclusion

The path to freelancing as a project manager is more possible now than ever. Get clear on the type of work you want to do and how you add value, then get out there and start networking. Good luck!

CHAPTER THREE

Tech-Forward Project Management: Mastering the Digital Landscape

By Dr. Tori R. Dodla

Emerging technologies[1] have allotted project managers new tools and software in the last decade. And not just for tracking projects, either. Today, organizations across all industries harness the power of digital tools to streamline processes, enhance collaboration, and achieve project success.

Tech-forward project management strategically uses technology, digital tools, and software to optimize project management processes. By embracing technology, new project managers can position themselves at the forefront of innovation and unlock new possibilities for success.

In my first project management role, I suffered, and I suffered greatly. Optimistic, I assumed that my PMP certification, tied in with my background was all that I needed to succeed.

---

1   Tools and software mentioned in this chapter are for informational purposes only and not advertisements.

My first formal project management job was at a hospital, in the patient records department. As an honest person, I let my supervisor know within the first month of working that I did not understand my role. I was drowning. Not only was I assigned an outrageous number of projects – 112 to be exact – but I did not feel effective or productive.

My supervisor told me to be patient and that everyone who comes from an industry outside of healthcare experiences "growing pains." Months went by and I felt like a complete failure and a glorified secretary. Most of my projects were cancelled, with only three reaching completion.

Eventually, my senior project manager attempted to micro-manage me; I was to report to his office every morning and give a status update on my projects. By then, I had already given up. Luckily, I found another role and moved on.

In those moments, it never occurred to me that I could use technology to maximize productivity, engage stakeholders, communicate with team members, or basically survive. Now I understand that in order to navigate the landscape of project management, it's important to harness whatever tools we have at our disposal. In this chapter, I share technology-driven recommendations and digital tools for the up-and-coming project manager.

Learn the Technical Language

After five years in the US Army, I would say things like, "I need this by COB" or "let's get a left seat, right seat, and an SOP today." I even remember sending an e-mail that began "ALCON." That e-mail prompted my manager to pull me aside and explain that I had to let go of my Army vocabulary. He was right.

But just as "Army speak" is code to the average civilian,

healthcare terminology and everything associated sounded like a different language to me. Not understanding the language of healthcare made meetings painful. And it made working with my developers even more painful.

Every industry has its own language. Learn all the technical language, jargon, and acronyms associated with your industry. It will return huge dividends, making you more competent and confident. This doesn't mean you must become a developer, but learn what an API is and why it's important to your project.

Project managers are at the forefront of managing complex initiatives often involving cross-functional teams, diverse stakeholders, and intricate technical processes. To effectively navigate these challenges, you really need to be fluent in the language of your industry.

Effective communication is the cornerstone of successful project management. For new project managers, gaining fluency in industry language is not just an asset, but a necessity.

Your main goal is to communicate with precision!

For example, ATM to the average person means automatic teller machine, but if you work in meteorology, ATM means atmosphere. However, if you are talking to a colleague on a Teams chat, ATM could mean "at this moment."

Understanding industry-specific terminology and technical vocabulary will allow you to communicate precisely. It eliminates ambiguity and misunderstanding, ensuring project goals, requirements, and expectations are accurately conveyed to team members and stakeholders. As a project manager, you will be taking and recording notes. It's very important that you speak your industry's language.

Also, you want to establish credibility and trust, leading to stronger working relationships and increased cooperation. Most project manager positions share resources, meaning developers often do not "belong" to a single project manager. If you find yourself in a situation where you will be competing for time, you want to appear as confident as possible.

Remember that effective project management involves satisfying the needs of various stakeholders, each with their own interests and priorities. Speaking their language demonstrates empathy, understanding, and a commitment to meeting their requirements. You should practice translating technical language back to common English to keep your stakeholders informed.

Here are some key facts to motivate you to learn technical and industry jargon:

- Misunderstandings resulting from miscommunication can lead to project delays, scope creep, and increased costs.

- A clear understanding of industry terminology will enable you, as a project manager, to make informed decisions. It facilitates critical thinking and weighing the pros and cons of various options.

- In the event of a problem, proficiency in industry language accelerates problem resolution by enabling efficient communication among team members and stakeholders.

Now, here are some strategies for learning technical and industry language with ease:

- Engage with industry professionals, attend conferences, and participate in workshops to gain exposure.

- Regularly read industry-specific publications, reports, and blogs to familiarize yourself with the language and stay updated on trends.

- Interact with colleagues and peers in your industry to

learn from their experiences and adopt their vocabulary.

- Get a mentor who can guide you in understanding the nuances of industry terminology.

- Read over past project documentation and research every term that you do not already know.

By investing in learning industry-specific and technical terminology, you will set yourself on a trajectory for success. Not only will you promote effective communication and collaboration, but you will enhance your professionalism and credibility and increase the likelihood of more opportunities.

Master Project Management Tools

While looking for subsequent project manager roles after my hospital project managemer debacle, I interviewed for *more* project management roles.

In one of my interviews, I was asked a particular question about Microsoft Project. Now, I never used Microsoft Project at the hospital as it wasn't available. However, I used Microsoft Project in school, so I put it on my resume like any rookie. During this interview, I was very embarrassed that not only could I not answer the question, but I did not remember anything from when I used it before.

Because there are many different types of project management tools available, I can't tell you which one to study. I suggest studying the one you put on your resume.

Regardless of the tool you use, this is where you want to start:

- Become very familiar with the interface. This includes ribbons, task panes, and various views. You want to know all of the basic functions and where they are located.

- Know everything you can about task scheduling, including task constraints, deadlines, and milestones.

- I can't express this enough that you must understand how to identify and manage the critical path in your project. I found this came up often in interviews.

- Finally, explore how to customize different project views, tables, and fields.

For new project managers, I highly suggest completing online demos for an opportunity to use project management tools on real-world examples. Not only is this a huge investment in your professional development, but becoming an expert on project management tools will weigh heavily on the success of the projects you manage.

What's in it for you? If you are still not convinced, then here are a few more reasons to really master your project management software. Becoming an expert on this software will:

- Help you to work more efficiently and accomplish tasks faster.

- Allow you to develop comprehensive and realistic project plans that set the team up for success.

- Enable you to optimize resource utilization and ensure tasks are completed on time.

- Let you leverage features like centralized communication, document sharing, and real-time updates to enhance team collaboration.

- Offer better visibility into project status, milestones, and potential roadblocks through project management tools.

- Enable informed decision-making and proactive issue resolution.

- Help you analyze project performance, identify trends, and make data-driven decisions to improve project outcomes.

- Prompt you to maintain an organized repository of project-related information for future reference.

- Allow you to be more adaptable to changing project requirements and circumstances and modify plans, adjust schedules, and reallocate resources efficiently.

- Enhance your skill set and be more marketable and valuable.

Learn the Technical Tasks of Each Team Member

Five months into my first project manager role, I visited one of my team members to get a demo of what he did in his role. It was eye-opening. I remember thinking "I wish I would have done this on my very first day." I would have been able to better understand my own role.

Understanding the roles and responsibilities of everyone on your project team is crucial. The worst position is to be in charge and not know the nuances of the roles that you lead.

But when you understand what each team member does, you can communicate more effectively. You can ask informed questions, provide clear instructions, and engage in meaningful discussions related to the work. Knowing team members' skills and expertise helps you assign tasks that match their strengths. This leads to improved task performance and overall project efficiency.

Furthermore, understanding team members' workload and availability helps you allocate resources more efficiently. This prevents overloading individuals and ensures balanced work distribution. Awareness of team members' roles allows you to identify potential bottlenecks or dependencies in the project. This helps in developing contingency plans and mitigating risks associated with team availability or expertise.

In complex projects, issues can arise that require quick problem-solving. Understanding team members' roles enables you to identify the right person to address specific challenges.

Recognizing and acknowledging team members' roles and contributions may indirectly foster a positive work environment. It shows that you value their expertise and are invested in their success.

Projects often involve cross-functional collaboration. Understanding the responsibilities of different team members helps facilitate smoother collaboration by promoting a common understanding of goals and expectations. When you understand what team members are capable of, you can delegate tasks more effectively. This reduces the chance that you have to micromanage, empowering team members to take ownership of their work.

Finally, understanding what each team member does allows you to identify areas for skill development, training, or process improvement within the team. Having a deep understanding of your team members' roles and responsibilities empowers you to lead more effectively, make informed decisions, and create an environment where everyone can contribute their best to the project's success.

Learn the Amount of Time Technical Tasks Take

I remember knocking on the cubicle of one of our developers to get an idea of her workload, intending to prioritize a project. After a few "umms" and "ahs," she gave me an estimate of how long it would take her to work on this new project and when she could start working. I walked away with an uneasy feeling; I felt like I had just made a deal with a car salesman.

Why must you know how long it takes everyone to do their job? While it may be impossible to know the times for sure, get an idea of how long it takes people to do their jobs so you can keep everyone working toward the project goals.

In addition, you don't want to be that project manager who promises impossible timelines to customers, expecting your developers to live up to your outrageous promises.

How do you do this?

- Review past project documentation and tasks completed by team members to gather historical data on task durations. This can serve as a baseline for estimating future tasks and projects.

- Google tutorials and watch YouTube Videos to get an understanding of specific tasks.

- Consult with freelancers in the same roles. Look up similar tasks and durations from people on Fiverr or Upwork. Talk to people on LinkedIn.

- Implement time-tracking software or tools that team members can use to log the time they spend on specific tasks.

Many project management software platforms have built-in time-tracking features. This will definitely help you benchmark re-occurring tasks for the future.

Use Technology to Improve Notetaking

I've always been proud of being a good note-taker and knowing what notes were important to take. Project management proved me wrong. At the end of every meeting, I realized how much information I missed and was nervous about how the lack of information would affect the project.

As a project manager, taking good meeting notes will be one of the most important things you can do. Note-taking is a fundamental practice for project managers to ensure effective communication, documentation, accountability, and decision-making throughout the project lifecycle. It serves as a valuable tool for managing the complexity and demands of project management effectively. Use technology to get help with notetaking:

- Record meetings so you can go back and review key points. Meeting recordings are a comprehensive and accurate record of what transpired during the meeting. This documentation can be crucial for reference, dispute resolution, and maintaining a clear historical record of project discussions and decisions. Meeting recordings can also be shared with team members who could not attend the meeting due to scheduling conflicts or other reasons. This ensures that absent team members stay informed about project updates and decisions.

- Use Otter.AI or other Voice-to-Text technology. Voice-to-text technology allows for the real-time transcription of spoken words into text. This means that meeting minutes and notes can be generated automatically during the meeting, reducing the need for manual notetaking and ensuring that a detailed record of the discussion is available immediately after the meeting concludes.

- Use meeting apps like Microsoft Teams, Zoom, or Google Meet, which often have built-in note-taking features or integrations with note-taking tools.

- Use software, such as Grammarly, to proofread your notes. You will thank yourself later for "going the extra mile." Proofreading software can quickly identify and highlight spelling and grammatical errors in written notes. This will help you ensure that your project notes are clear, professional, and free of language-related mistakes.

- Use tagging and metadata features in your note-taking tools or document management systems to categorize and search for notes quickly. Tags can help you classify notes by project, topic, or date.

- Choose document management tools with robust search functionality, allowing you to find specific notes or information quickly. Advanced search options can save time when you need to retrieve specific details.

Automate What You Can

As a project manager, scheduling meetings, following up with people, and checking on tasks left me feeling like a glorified secretary. I never had enough time for anything, and I almost always forgot the "little things."

Here are a few reasons why you should automate what you can:

- Automation eliminates manual and repetitive tasks, allowing you to allocate your time and energy to more strategic and value-added activities. This can significantly improve your overall productivity.

- Automated processes reduce the risk of human error. Computers and software follow predefined rules consistently, reducing the likelihood of mistakes in task execution and data entry.

- Automation ensures that tasks are performed consistently according to established standards and workflows. This consistency contributes to better project outcomes and compliance with project plans.

- Automation tools can collect and analyze data, providing valuable insights into project performance and trends. This data-driven approach enhances decision-making and project optimization.

Here are 8 things you can automate:

1. **Task assignment and tracking.** Use project management software to automatically assign tasks to team members based on predefined criteria or workflows. Set up task dependencies and automated notifications to inform team members of task updates and deadlines.

2. **Time tracking.** As mentioned before, implement time-tracking tools or software to automate the collection of hours worked by team members on specific tasks. Use these tools to generate reports on time spent and compare them against planned estimates.

3. **Communication.** Schedule automated reminders and notifications for meetings, deadlines, or project milestones. Make it a habit to be punctual in all of your meetings. Use e-mail templates or chatbots to automate routine communication with team members or stakeholders.

4. **Reporting and dashboards.** Set up automated reporting tools to generate regular project status reports, including key performance indicators and progress updates. If necessary, create automated dashboards that provide real-time visibility into project metrics.

5. **Client and stakeholder communication.** Automate client or stakeholder communication through project portals or client management tools. Send automated project updates or status reports to stakeholders.

6. **Knowledge sharing.** Implement knowledge management systems to automate the collection and dissemination of project-related knowledge and lessons learned. Use automated tagging and categorization for easy retrieval.

7. **Performance evaluation.** Automate performance evaluations and feedback collection for team members through performance management tools. Generate automated performance reports for team assessment and improvement.

8. **Post-project evaluation.** Finally, automate post-project evaluation surveys and data collection to gather feedback and insights for continuous improvement.

Embrace the Future of Project Management in the Digital Age

Get ready for the future. As organizations across industries adapt to the demands of the digital age, project management practices are evolving to harness the power of technology for improved efficiency, collaboration, and innovation.

Organizations are integrating digital technologies into every facet of their operations. Project management is no exception, with digital tools and platforms reshaping how projects are planned, executed, and monitored. In addition, the influx of data from various sources drives the adoption of data analytics and AI in project management.

Always continue learning. This doesn't mean you have to get a bunch of unnecessary certifications that have nothing to do with your current project management job. This means being open to learning more about the tools that you interact with daily.

It won't hurt to be "forward-thinking." When applying for project manager jobs, conduct an assessment gap and learn new technologies that get you an interview and bridge over into the next role.

Embracing the future of project management in the digital age is not just a choice but a necessity for all project managers to remain competitive. The convergence of technology, data analytics, and agile practices empowers project managers and teams to confidently navigate complex challenges.

By harnessing the benefits of digital tools and cultivating a forward-looking mindset, you will seize the opportunities presented by the digital age and embark on a path of sustainable growth and innovation in project management.

As technology continues to evolve, mastering the digital landscape is an ongoing pursuit that promises to help you revolutionize project management and shape a more agile, efficient, and innovative future.

CHAPTER FOUR

Project Manager Authority and the Affect It Has on Project Manager Stress

By Dr. Max Boller

In today's fast-paced business environment, projects are the driving force behind achieving strategic goals. And at the heart of these projects are project managers, the individuals responsible for steering the ship through the complexities of project management. But what makes a project manager's role truly impactful is the level of authority they hold.

Authority isn't a one-size-fits-all concept. It varies depending on the organization's culture, the specific demands of a project, and the industry landscape. This authority, encompassing decision-making autonomy, control over resources, and the ability to set directions, can significantly shape a project manager's experience on the job.

On one hand, having more authority can make decision-making smoother and provide flexibility. Yet it also brings increased responsibility, often leading to feelings of isolation and burnout. There's a delicate balance to strike.

This delicate balance between authority and stress is the focus of this chapter. We're going to dive deep into the intricate relationship between a project manager's authority and the stress they contend with. We'll explore the dimensions of authority, uncover the stressors that project managers commonly face – such as role ambiguity, resource constraints, interpersonal conflicts, time pressures, and organizational politics – and we'll discuss strategies to find that sweet spot of authority where project managers can thrive.[1]

Throughout this chapter we will navigate the ever-evolving world of project management, shedding light on how PMs can effectively harness their authority, ensuring successful project delivery while skillfully managing the inevitable stress that comes with the territory.[2]

The Nature of Project Manager Authority

Let's break down the essence of a project manager's authority. It's not just some generic term; it's a multifaceted concept that's absolutely vital for the success of any project. So, what's this authority all about, and why does it matter so much? When we talk about a project manager's authority, we're essentially diving into the realm of power, autonomy,

---

[1] Flannes, S. (2010). Tangible tips for handling the endless stress in project management. Paper presented at the PMI® Global Congress 2010—North America.

[2] Wu, G., Hu, Z., & Zheng, J. (2019). Role stress, job burnout, and job performance in construction project managers: The moderating role of career calling. *International Journal of Environmental Research and Public Health*, 16(13).

Authority and Project Manager Stress   55

and responsibility.[3] These three elements are like the pillars holding up the whole project management structure.

First, there's power. Now, don't think of it as a power trip or something along those lines. It's more about the PM's ability to influence decisions, rally the troops, and sometimes make those tough calls that can make or break a project. It's not just about being the boss within the team; it's also about having sway with stakeholders, vendors, and even clients.[4]

Next up, we've got autonomy. This is all about freedom. The PM needs space to make decisions without having to go through layers of approvals. It covers everything from budget choices to resource allocations. Autonomy lets the project manager act fast, based on their expertise and understanding of what the project needs. In environments where red tape slows things down, having this freedom not only speeds things up but also shows that the organization trusts the project manager's skills.[5]

And with power and autonomy comes responsibility. It's not just about being accountable for the end result. It's a constant process of making sure every decision aligns with the project's goals and the bigger picture of the organization. It's about answering to teams, stakeholders, and the whole organization to ensure resources are used wisely, risks are managed, and the project stays on track. In a way, the PM's responsibility is similar to a tightrope act, balancing between the power they

---

3   Stickney, F. A. & Johnston, W. R. (1983). Delegation and a sharing of authority by the project manager. *Project Management Quarterly,* 14(1), 42–53.

4   Zaleznik, A. (1970). Power and politics in organizational life (pp. 47–60). Harvard Business School Publishing.

5   Kumar, V. S. (2009). Essential leadership skills for project managers. Paper presented at PMI® Global Congress 2009—North America, Orlando, FL. Newtown Square, PA: Project Management Institute.

have, the freedom they enjoy, and the project's overall objectives.[6]

Now, here's the twist. These elements of PM authority can look quite different depending on the organization and the project. In big, bureaucratic setups, project managers might have less autonomy due to the sheer complexity of things. But in startups or smaller teams, they might have a lot more freedom to wear many hats and steer the ship on their own.

No matter how you slice it, understanding the nature of PM authority is key. It sets the tone for how a project unfolds, influences team dynamics, and determines how adaptable and resilient a project can be when faced with challenges.

Remember, project manager authority isn't just a fancy term. It's the secret ingredient that makes project management work. Recognizing its intricacies and implications is crucial for empowering project managers, aligning project goals, and creating an environment where projects can run like well-oiled machines.

Navigating the Dimensions of Authority in Project Management

Let's take a closer look at the various facets of authority in project management. While project management is all about planning, executing, and closing projects, it's also about managing authority effectively to overcome the numerous challenges that come your way.

Authority, in the realm of project management, isn't a one-size-fits-all concept; it's a multi-dimensional, ever-shifting

---

[6] Gemuenden, Hans & Salomo, Sören & Krieger, Axel. (2005). The Influence of Project Autonomy on Project Success. *International Journal of Project Management* - INT J PROJ MANAG. 23. 366-373.

landscape. These dimensions are not just abstract concepts; they're the very bedrock upon which a project manager's strategies and adaptability are built. There exist three fundamental dimensions of authority that govern a project manager's journey: decision-making autonomy, resource control, and direction setting.

In my own professional journey, I've had the privilege (and sometimes the challenge) of experiencing the full spectrum of these authority dimensions. Picture this: I've led projects where I was the unequivocal shot-caller. When a game-changing $250,000 change order landed on my desk, the weight of deciding whether to greenlight it, back it with a compelling case for additional funds, or keep the project on its original course rested squarely on my shoulders. The exhilaration of autonomy mingled with the pressure to make the right call made those moments unforgettable.

However, I've also found myself on the polar opposite of this spectrum. I've been in situations where my authority seemed to evaporate into thin air, as if I were a mere puppet in a higher-up's grand production. In these instances, my role felt more akin to a coordinator, executing directives without the power to influence decisions. What added to the complexity was that concurrently, I might be overseeing other projects where I held the reins of authority firmly in my grasp. The mental gymnastics of switching between these authority levels, sometimes within the same hour, proved to be an unparalleled test of adaptability.

Navigating this fluctuating landscape of authority can be mentally taxing. The adrenaline rush of autonomy can give way to the frustration of powerlessness, all within the span of a single project cycle. However, it's precisely this dynamism that keeps the world of project management engaging and continually challenges us to refine our leadership skills.

Authority in project management isn't a static attribute but a dynamic interplay of decision-making, resource control, and direction setting. It's a multi-dimensional puzzle that every project manager must master, adapting to the circumstances at hand while striving to strike that delicate balance between control and coordination.

Starting with *decision-making autonomy*, this is where the project manager's role truly comes to life. How much freedom does a project manager have to make decisions without needing approval from higher-ups or external stakeholders? It varies widely across different organizations. Some PMs operate in environments with strict decision-making processes, while others have more latitude to act independently. Having more autonomy undoubtedly speeds up decision-making, cutting through red tape and delays.[7]

However, this freedom comes with its own set of challenges. With great autonomy comes greater responsibility for the project's outcomes. Successes become personal triumphs, but failures weigh heavily on the project manager's shoulders. The balance between autonomy and accountability depends on organizational culture, project nature, and the project manager's experience.

Next is *resource control*. This dimension gets into the nuts and bolts of project execution. Every project relies on resources, whether it's skilled personnel, financial capital, tools, or time. The project manager's ability to manage and allocate these resources is crucial. Can the project manager freely shift resources as project needs change, or are they constrained by predetermined allocations? Resource control allows the project manager to adapt quickly to unexpected challenges, ensur-

---

[7] Parth, F. R. (2013). Critical decision-making skills for project managers. Paper presented at PMI® Global Congress 2013—EMEA, Istanbul, Turkey. Newtown Square, PA: Project Management Institute.

ing the project stays on course.[8]

However, resource reallocation isn't always smooth sailing. In constrained environments, shifting resources can stir up conflicts. It requires not just strategic thinking but also excellent interpersonal skills to communicate decisions effectively and empathetically.

Finally, there's *direction setting*. Projects are dynamic, and the external and internal landscapes can shift. Does the project manager have the authority to change the project's course based on new information, unforeseen challenges, or shifting priorities? Being able to adjust the project's direction is a powerful tool. It ensures the project stays aligned with its objectives, even if the path changes. Like a ship's captain navigating storms, the project manager must sometimes alter the course to ensure a successful project outcome.

However, changing direction isn't straightforward. It can involve significant adjustments in resources, timelines, stakeholder expectations, and project goals. This can create uncertainty, demanding not only decisiveness but also top-notch communication skills to explain the reasons behind the shift and keep stakeholders committed.[9]

Project manager authority isn't a one-dimensional concept. It's a complex blend of decision-making autonomy, resource control, and direction setting. Each dimension presents opportunities and challenges. A project manager's effectiveness isn't just about the authority they have; it's about how wisely they use it. Balancing these dimensions requires a mix of strategic thinking, adaptability, and exceptional interpersonal skills,

---

8   Stickney, F. A. & Johnston, W. R. (1983). Delegation and a sharing of authority by the project manager. *Project Management Quarterly,* 14(1), 42-53.

9   Morris, P. W. G. & DeLapp, S. E. (1983). Managing change through project management. *Project Management Quarterly,* 14(2), 60-70.

making project management both an art and a science.

Understanding Stress Dynamics in Project Management

It's important to understand the world of *stress* in project management. It's a highly rewarding field, no doubt, but it's also filled with its fair share of challenges. And one of the big ones? Stress.

The nature of managing diverse teams, handling significant resources, and steering projects toward the finish line on tight schedules makes stress a pretty common companion for project managers. But before we get into how authority fits into this stress puzzle; we need to dissect the primary sources of stress for project managers.[10]

First, there is *role ambiguity*. Imagine being in charge of a project, but you're not entirely sure what your role entails. It's like trying to navigate a ship without a map. This ambiguity can stem from various sources, like unclear project objectives, lack of communication from higher-ups, or rapidly changing project dynamics. When a project manager doesn't know exactly what's expected, they might end up second-guessing their decisions, which can waste time and resources, or even send the project in the wrong direction. And here's the kicker: this uncertainty doesn't just mess with the project manager; it

---

10   Himmich, A. (2023, April 13). *Stress in Project Management: Causes, Effects, and Coping Strategies.* Retrieved from Linkedin.com: https://www.linkedin.com/pulse/stress-project-management-causes-effects-coping-anass-himmich/

can throw the whole project into chaos.[11]

Next are *resource constraints*. Every project, big or small, has limits when it comes to resources. Think limited staff, tight budgets, or not having the right tools and tech. Balancing the project's success within these constraints is like walking a tightrope. project managers have to constantly juggle, trying to get the most out of what's available without pushing too hard and risking burnout or project delays. It's a constant tug-of-war that can pile on the stress.[12]

Then there are *interpersonal dynamics*. Working with others is a big part of project management, and sometimes, those interactions can be like walking through a minefield. Conflicts with team members, stakeholders, or clients can be a huge source of stress. These conflicts can arise from differences in vision, disagreements over resource allocation, or even personal clashes. If these conflicts aren't dealt with, they can lead to project delays, lower quality work, and a generally unpleasant work environment.[13] Managing these interpersonal challenges while keeping the project on track takes a ton of skill and emotional intelligence and can be a major source of stress.

Time pressures are another stress factor. Projects often come with tight deadlines, and sometimes those deadlines get even tighter due to unforeseen challenges or changes in scope. Racing against the clock, making sure everything goes as planned – it can be incredibly pressure-packed. This can

---

11   Wu, G., Hu, Z., & Zheng, J. (2019). Role stress, job burnout, and job performance in construction project managers: The moderating role of career calling. *International Journal of Environmental Research and Public Health*, 16(13). doi.org/10.3390/ijerph16132394

12   Jackson, A.T. & Frame, M.C. (2018). Stress, health, and job performance: what do we know? *Journal of Applied Biobehavioral Research*. doi.org/10.1111/jabr.12147

13   Minavand, H., Reza, M., Tabrizi, F., Mohamed, S., & Baqutayan, S. (2013). The sources of job stress among project managers. *Research on Humanities and Social Sciences*, 3(16), 94-100.

lead to longer work hours, less downtime, and, of course, more stress.[14]

Finally, we can't leave out *organizational politics*. Projects don't exist in a vacuum; they're part of a bigger organizational picture. There are power dynamics, competing interests, and rivalries between departments.

Navigating these political waters, making sure the project doesn't get caught in the crossfire while serving various stakeholder interests, requires some serious political savvy. It's not just about getting the project done; it's about making sure it aligns with the broader goals and dynamics of the organization. That's another layer of complexity and stress for PMs to handle.[15]

Now, where does authority fit into all of this? Well, it's a significant factor, but it's just one piece of the puzzle. To effectively manage stress in project management, you have to understand all of these sources, from role ambiguity to organizational politics. Once you've got a handle on that, you can start developing strategies to deal with them. Recognizing these dynamics is the first step toward equipping both organizations and PMs with the tools and strategies they need to navigate the challenging, yet rewarding, world of project management.

Authority in Project Management: The Balance Between Empowerment and Stress

Now we need to look at the *authority* in project management, where it's a bit of a double-edged sword. On one side, it empowers project managers with the autonomy and

---

14 Michie, S. (2002). Causes and management of stress at work. *Occupational and Environmental Medicine*, 59(1), 67–72. doi.org/10.1136/oem.59.1.67
15 Michie (2002), 'Causes and management of stress at work' (n 15).

flexibility they need to steer projects to success. But on the flip side, this increased authority also comes with added responsibility, which can crank up stress levels. Understanding this intricate dance between authority and stress is the key to optimizing project outcomes and maintaining a positive work environment.[16]

Benefits of Having More Authority

Why do we even care about having more authority in project management? Well, it's like having a superpower. For project managers, one of the most obvious perks is smoother decision-making. With more authority, project managers can cut through the bureaucratic red tape and make important decisions quickly. No more waiting around for approvals. They can make critical calls on the spot, keeping the project on track and giving the team a sense of momentum and purpose.[17]

But it doesn't stop at decision-making. Having more authority also means having greater control over resources. And that's a game-changer in the ever-evolving world of projects. Think about it—projects change, face unexpected hurdles, and present new opportunities. Being able to adapt swiftly is pure gold.

Project managers with the right authority can shuffle resources around, whether it's people, funds, or materials. This agility ensures the project stays nimble. For example, if one

---

16 Mac Donald, K., Rezania, D., & Baker, R. (2020). A grounded theory examination of project managers' accountability. *International Journal of Project Management*, 38(1), 27-35.

17 Kain, J., & Jex, S. (2010). Karasek's (1979) job demands-control model: A summary of current issues and recommendations for future research. *Research in occupational stress and well-being (Vol. 8)*. Emerald Group Publishing. doi.org/10.1108/S1479-3555(2010)0000008009

phase hits a snag, a project manager with the necessary authority can quickly shift resources to tackle the issue, keeping disruptions to a minimum.

Moreover, having more authority lets PMs steer the project in the right direction. Big, complex projects often encounter situations where the initial plan doesn't cut it anymore. Project managers, armed with insights, expertise, and real-world knowledge, are best equipped to spot when a course correction is needed. With the right authority, they can guide the project toward a new path that aligns better with emerging data, stakeholder feedback, or external changes. This proactive approach keeps the project relevant, feasible, and on track to meet its objectives, even when the external landscape shifts.[18]

Challenges That Come with Authority

Now, let's talk about the challenges that come with great power. While more autonomy streamlines decision-making, it also means every decision's weight rests squarely on the project manager's shoulders. Making the call is liberating, but it also means taking full responsibility for the consequences. Resource allocation, while flexible, can also be a balancing act. Project managers need to ensure they distribute resources evenly and avoid conflicts or resource shortages. Steering the project's direction means staying on high alert for every little shift and making sure all stakeholders stay on board. It's like navigating a ship through constantly changing waters.

---

18   Smith, D. C., Bruyns, M., & Evans, S. (2011). A project manager's optimism and stress management and IT project success. *International Journal of Managing Projects in Business*, 4(1), 10-27. doi.org/10.1108/1753837111109683

The Authority-Stress Connection

In the end, authority can be a game-changer in project management, making projects more agile and adaptive. But it's a double-edged sword. More authority means more responsibility and potential stressors. The secret sauce for organizations and project managers is finding the right balance. It's about recognizing that authority has its pros and cons and figuring out how to make the most of the good stuff while minimizing the challenges. With the right mix, authority can indeed become a powerful tool for excellence in project management.

Navigating the Hurdles of Having More Authority in Project Management

In the world of project management, having more authority is often seen as a golden ticket to efficiency, freedom, and confident decision-making. But, just like any tool, it can be a both good and bad. Elevated authority, while offering a ton of perks, also brings its fair share of challenges that, if not handled well, can trip up a project manager both professionally and personally.[19]

The Burden of Responsibility. One of the biggest challenges that comes with having more authority is the added responsibility. You know that old saying, "with great power comes great responsibility"? Well, it's spot-on for project management. When a project manager has more authority, they're entrusted with making some serious decisions – from

---

19 Sauer, C., Liu, L., & Johnston, K. (2001). Where Project Managers are Kings. *Project Management Journal*, 32(4), 39–49. https://doi.org/10.1177/875697280103200406

the money stuff to where resources go and even changing the direction of the whole project. It's empowering, no doubt, but it also means the project manager is the go-to person if things go south. Successes get cheered on, but slip-ups? They land squarely on the decision-maker's plate. This level of accountability can heap a ton of pressure on the project manager. Every choice they make can swing the project in a big way. This responsibility, especially in high-stakes projects, can be a major stress factor. The project manager is basically under a microscope, with every call they make under intense scrutiny.[20]

The Loneliness of the Decision-Maker. Here's another tricky challenge that often flies under the radar – isolation. When project managers have a ton of authority, they're often perched at the top of the decision-making pyramid. It sounds great, right? Well, it can be a lonely place. Why? Because the big calls, especially the crucial ones, often need to be made solo, without the luxury of bouncing ideas around with a group. This solo decision-making can lead to feelings of isolation. The project manager might feel disconnected from their team, their peers, or even other folks involved in the project. This emotional distance can have ripple effects. It can lead to potential blind spots in decision-making and even mess with the project manager's mental health, making them feel like they're on their own little island.[21]

The Burnout Factor. And let's not forget about burnout.

---

20   Kumar, V. S. (2009). Essential leadership skills for project managers. Paper presented at PMI® Global Congress 2009—North America, Orlando, FL. Newtown Square, PA: Project Management Institute.

21   Biafore, B. (2023, September 5). What If You Feel Lonely as a PM. Retrieved from LinkedIn.com: https://www.linkedin.com/pulse/what-you-feel-lonely-pm-bonnie-biafore#:~:text=If%20you're%20feeling%20lonely,and%20apply%20some%20practical%20steps

It's a biggie. The never-ending cycle of decision-making, day in and day out, can take a real toll on the brain. Every choice, no matter how small, eats up brainpower. Over time, this constant mental grind, combined with the pressure of being accountable and the potential isolation, can lead to burnout. Burnout isn't just bad for the project manager's well-being; it can also throw a wrench into project outcomes. A burnt-out project manager might start slowing down, making fuzzier decisions, and might not be as responsive to the project's needs.[22]

Having more authority in project management comes with some amazing perks, but it's no walk in the park. The heavy responsibility, possible feelings of isolation, and the looming burnout threat make up the trio of challenges that come with the territory. Recognizing these hurdles is the first step to tackling them. Organizations and PMs themselves need to be aware of these potential pitfalls. They should have systems in place to offer support, promote connectivity, and safeguard mental well-being. Only then can the full potential of authority be tapped into, blending empowerment with empathy, and decisiveness with personal wellness.

Discovering the Right Balance: Authority in Project Management

In the intricate world of project management, authority isn't just a fancy term; it's a critical factor that can make or break a project manager's performance, well-being, and stress levels. Picture it as a delicate dance – too little authority, and

---

22 Pinto, J. K., Dawood, S., & Pinto, M. B. (2014). Project management and burnout: Implications of the Demand-Control-Support model on project-based work. *International Journal of Project Management*, 32(4), 578–589. doi.org/10.1016/j.ijproman.2013.09.003

the project manager might feel handcuffed, unable to steer the project effectively. But give them too much authority, and it's like a heavy cloak that can lead to decision fatigue, isolation, and burnout. The real challenge is to find that sweet spot, that optimal level of authority – not too much, not too little, but just right – empowering project managers without overwhelming them.[23]

Understanding the Optimal Level of Authority

Think of the ideal, or optimal, authority level like the perfect balance of a swinging pendulum. At this equilibrium, project managers have enough power to make decisions, allocate resources, and steer the ship without feeling like they're on an isolated decision-making island. They can respond to the project's changing needs while avoiding the trap of getting bogged down in every tiny detail, which could lead to decision fatigue and, ultimately, burnout.[24]

The Crucial Role of Organizational Support

Getting to this optimal authority level isn't a solo mission. Organizations have a big part to play in creating an environment where this balance can thrive. It all starts with tailored training programs for project managers. These programs should equip them with the skills needed to handle increased authority effectively – things like decision-making frame-

---

23 Labrosse, M. (2013, August 26). *5 ways project managers use power.* Retrieved from projectmanager.com.au: https://projectmanager.com.au/5-ways-project-managers-use-power/

24 Li, S., & Weng, X. (2017). Random authority. *International Economic Review, 58*(1), 211-235.

works, leadership techniques, stakeholder management, and even strategies for stress relief.

But it doesn't stop at training. Support systems are a game-changer. Imagine mentorship programs where seasoned project managers share their wisdom with less-experienced ones, helping them navigate the tricky waters of authority. Plus, organizations can provide access to counseling or mental well-being resources to ensure that project managers have a way to address stress or feelings of isolation when they arise.

Delegation: Your Secret Weapon for Balance

Here's a powerful tool in the quest for balance: delegation. Authority doesn't mean the project manager needs to do every single thing themselves. By entrusting tasks and responsibilities to team members, project managers can lighten their own workload and give their team members a sense of ownership and involvement in the project's success.

But here's the kicker – effective delegation hinges on trust. project managers need to trust their team's capabilities and know how to match tasks with the right skill sets. When that trust is reciprocated by team members who deliver on their responsibilities, it reinforces the collaborative nature of the project and reduces the potential for project manager isolation.

The Influence of Feedback Loops

In the journey toward optimal authority, feedback is your guiding star. Regular feedback programs, whether they're formal or informal, bridge the gap between project managers and their teams, stakeholders, or clients. Constructive feedback can boost a project manager's confidence, letting them know they're on the right track. It also helps pinpoint areas that need improvement, steering the project back on course when necessary.

But feedback goes beyond tactics; it plays a psychological role. It fights feelings of isolation, reminding project managers that they're not alone in their journey. They're part of a team effort, with every contribution shaping the project's success.

The Ever-Changing Balance

Optimal authority in project management isn't a one-size-fits-all kind of thing. It's a dynamic balance, influenced by the project's nature, the project manager's personality, and the organization's culture. While the exact balance might shift from one scenario to another, the principles stay the same: equip project managers with the skills to handle authority, create a supportive and collaborative environment, and maintain a feedback loop. Achieving this balance not only drives project success but also fosters a positive, engaged, and sustainable work environment.

Fictional Illustration Case Study: The Authority-Stress Nexus in Project Management

Company Snapshot: Meet EdgeTech Inc., a big-shot global IT solutions company. They handle all sorts of projects every year, from small tech tweaks to massive infrastructure makeovers.

Jane's Challenge: Now, there's Jane, a seasoned project manager at EdgeTech Inc. They handed her this high-stakes project, and it was a big deal. The company said, "Hey Jane, you're in charge of everything – call the shots, control the resources, and steer the ship."

The Ups and Downs: At first, Jane was thrilled. She could make decisions in a snap without waiting for a pile of approvals. But as time passed, she started feeling the downside of all that power. The constant decision-making, dealing with team conflicts, and trying to meet crazy deadlines were wearing her out. Jane felt like she was on her own island, and the fear of burning out was creeping in.

The Authority-Stress Puzzle: Jane's situation was like a real-life example of what we've heard about in studies. Her supercharged authority was a mixed bag. It made things run smoother, but it also piled on stress, loneliness, and a ton of responsibility. Meanwhile, her colleagues who managed projects with less authority had their own set of issues. They were stuck with unclear roles and had to ask for approvals all the time, which led to project delays.

The Fix: To help Jane out, EdgeTech Inc. decided to take some action:

1. **Institutional Support.** They hooked her up with a mentor – a bigwig who'd been in Jane's shoes before. This mentor gave her advice, a listening ear, and some direction when she needed it.

2. **Effective Delegation.** Jane went through some training on delegation. She started passing off certain decision-making tasks to her deputy managers and team leaders. This not only lightened her load but also gave

her team more power and made things more collaborative.

3. **Feedback Time.** They started having regular meetings where Jane and her team could chat about the project, share their worries, and offer insights. This made Jane feel less alone and helped her make better decisions.

The Outcome: After these changes, Jane's stress levels dropped big time. With the mix of mentorship, delegation, and regular feedback, she could handle her authority without getting crushed by the pressure. And those with less authority? Well, they got clearer roles and stopped holding up projects.

Key Lessons: EdgeTech Inc.'s experience taught them a few lessons. When it comes to giving power to project managers, it's all about balance. Too much or too little can mess things up for both the projects and the managers themselves. By spotting the warning signs early and making some smart moves, companies can make sure their project managers are ready to handle the craziness, and everyone comes out on top.

Striking the Right Balance Between Authority and Well-being in Project Management

As we navigate the complex world of project management, one thing stands out – the authority given to project managers is a blessing and a potential curse, all rolled into one. Our study has shed light on this dual nature of authority. On one hand, it's the key to streamlining operations, making things run like a well-oiled machine. But on the other hand, it can put immense pressure on project managers, leading to stressors like isolation and burnout.

Authority and Project Manager Stress   73

Let's face it, project managers have their plates full of challenges. From dealing with role ambiguity to wading through the murky waters of organizational politics, there are no easy tasks. And guess what? All these challenges get magnified based on the level of authority they hold.

But don't worry, as this chapter has uncovered, there is a glimmer of hope – an optimal authority level, a sweet spot, if you will. This balance ensures that project managers have enough power to make those crucial decisions without drowning in a pool of responsibilities. It's not a stroke of luck; it takes structured interventions to get there.

Who plays a crucial role in this quest for balance? Organizations, that's who. They need to step up with institutional support, cultivate a culture of delegation, and keep those feedback mechanisms humming. These are the non-negotiables.

To sum it all up, authority is like a trusty tool in the project manager's toolkit. But here's the catch – it needs to be wielded wisely, and that's where robust organizational frameworks come in. Only then can project managers achieve the dual goal of delivering projects with finesse while keeping their well-being intact. It's all about striking that harmonious chord between authority and stress management.

CHAPTER FIVE

De Facto vs. *De Jure* Projects

By Joseph Jordan

No dilemma frustrates more than trying to enter a career field that requires prior experience with no way to gain said experience other than working in that career field.

Project management is one of those career fields. Organizations do not hire employees for this critical role without experience already in hand. At least, not for positions that actually include the title of *project manager*. Which makes sense. You would not want a doctor treating you who does not already have medical experience. Exemplary soft skills will not lead to being prescribed the correct medicine or execution of a successful surgical procedure.

But doctors get training in school and spend years under strict supervision through internships to claim the medical experience needed to be considered a doctor upon graduation. There is no such support infrastructure for project managers in most parts of the world, or outside of the largest project-oriented organizations.

So, what to do?

If you are a knowledge worker or a manager of any kind, undoubtedly your weeks and workdays are filled with tasks that need to be accomplished. Many tasks are simple and repetitive, so much so that you hardly notice them. They become part of your organization's operations, like closing payroll or submitting a weekly status report.

Other tasks may be more complicated. Perhaps you execute them in response to a specific trigger. For example, any change to normal procedures that you implement to improve operations would be such a task.

Let us examine this latter category more closely. You may believe even these tasks can be completed without much preparation, just a job that needs to be done. But it may turn out that some of these tasks could benefit from planning.

What if you chose to transform one of these tasks into a small project? An informal project.

De Jure and *De Facto* Projects

I have coined the terms *de facto* project and *de jure* project to distinguish between formal and informal projects. Here are what I consider to be the differences:

- **De Jure Project.** A project as most people define it, one that an organization starts – usually through a charter that is signed off by an executive sponsor – with a specific scope, a forecasted schedule, and an allotted budget for resources. Usually, a *de jure* project is managed by a full-time project manager. This person is responsible only for monitoring and controlling the execution of the project, not for carrying out the work itself.

- **De Facto Project.** A task executed within an organization that someone transforms into a project by creating a charter that describes the purpose of the task (whether signed off by an executive sponsor or not), by developing a schedule, and by monitoring the resources used to complete the task. Frequently, a *de facto* project is managed by a project manager who also contributes to the work itself. Sometimes the *de facto* project manager is the only contributor.

The most important feature of the *de facto* project is that someone who takes the time and effort to transform that task into a project.

Coud that someone be you?

If you do accept this challenge, there are benefits – but there is something you must understand: transforming a task into a project creates overhead, additional work you would not need to carry out if you merely executed the task and were done with it.

I will explain what that extra work looks like in a bit, but let us first explore those benefits I mentioned. I like to call them *the three P's*:

- **Practice.** Even if a task does not require planning, by doing so you learn how to follow a schedule and how to control the cost of the work required to complete the scope of the task. This practice will prepare you for project management when you are assigned to manage true projects one day.

- **Proof.** By transforming your tasks into *de facto* projects, and documenting the planning and execution of these projects, you prove that you have project management skills and experience. You can use this experience to achieve advancements into project management roles within your current organization, or to apply for project management opportunities elsewhere.

- **PMP.** The Project Management Professional (PMP) is the flagship certification for the Project Management Institute (PMI) and is the most sought-after certification for project managers around the world. To apply for this certification, you must first demonstrate that you have 60 months of experience leading projects (or 36 months if you have a four-year university degree). You can demonstrate that you meet this requirement by converting tasks you have performed in the past into *de facto* projects.

In classical project management terminology, a project is generally considered to have three components, *scope* (the reason for the project in the first place), *time* (the duration required to achieve the scope, often divided into schedule activities and milestones), and *cost* (the price of the labor, material, and service resources required to achieve the scope).

If you consider that a task has three simple components, *requirement*, *execution*, and *outcome*, you could say that the scope of the task goes from requirement to outcome, with execution of the task incurring a cost over the time of the schedule. As mentioned earlier, for simple tasks you would not usually think about this association between a task and project management concepts. But by transforming the task into a *de facto* project, you must make this association.

And now for the additional work I warned you about. To prove you are managing a task like a project, you must *plan*, *monitor*, and *close*. This means you must plan what you anticipate the schedule and cost of the project to be; you must monitor the progress of achieving the scope and the actual cost incurred over the project schedule duration; and - upon closing the *de facto* project - document whether or not you successfully achieved the scope, how long it actually took, and how much it actually cost, compared to what you had planned.

Do not worry. The extra work I outlined above may seem like, well - a lot of extra work! But I will now describe the minimal amount of effort you need to prove you have project management experience. Remember, this lesson is about what to do if you have unilaterally decided to transform an assigned task into a *de facto* project. If your supervisor, or anyone else in a leadership position within your organization has instructed you to manage the task as though it was a project, they may have their own ideas on how to plan, monitor, and - most importantly - document the project's execution.

Chartering: Project Authorization and Initiation

There are many resources out there - both free and available for purchase (at a multitude of price points and in a multitude of formats) - to instruct you on how to manage a project. PMI publishes a *Guide to the Project Management Body of Knowledge (PMBOK) and The Standard for Project Management* (currently on the Seventh Edition as I write this), which - as the name implies - is a globally-recognized standard on how to manage projects.

This combined publication (a free download for PMI members) does not provide a straightforward methodology to transform a task into a *de facto* project. But there is one artifact prescribed by the PMI and most authorities on project management that I believe is indispensable and should be the first item developed at the beginning of any project - *de facto* or *de jure* - and that is the *project charter*.

According to the PMBOK, a project charter (which I will

simply refer to as *charter* from here on out) "is a document issued by the project initiator or sponsor that formally authorizes the existence of a project and provides the project manager with the authority to apply organizational resources to project activities."

By this definition, for a *de facto* project, you would be both the project manager and the project initiator. We will assume for the moment that, if you have been given a task to complete, then you already have the authority to apply organizational resources to carry out that task. But unlike a *de jure* project that should have a project sponsor to sign off on a charter, there is most likely no identified project sponsor for a *de facto* project.

Since I propose that you develop a charter for every task that you decide to transform into a project, I also recommend that you ask your supervisor - or any other leader within your organization - to sign and approve your charters for *de facto* projects before you start the work.

Usually, a *de jure* project would have a project management plan. For a small *de facto* project, the charter could serve this purpose. If you prefer to create such a plan - separate from the charter - that is up to you.

There are many examples and templates available on the web on how to develop and maintain a project management plan. For now, let us proceed assuming that a charter will serve the function of a project management plan for your *de facto* project.

Working Within the Project Management Triangle

To achieve the three P's (practice, proof, and PMP), there is a minimum amount of information and specific data that must be in your charter. This data includes scope, time, and cost, the three constraints that make up the *project management triangle*.

- **Scope.** This is what your project is about, the requirement that results in some sort of outcome, and all the things that must be done to achieve that outcome. In a traditional project management plan, the scope would be described within a *work breakdown structure (WBS)*. For a *de facto* project, there is no need for anything as formal as a WBS, but you must document the requirement, the desired outcome (which could be an update to a process or procedure, a new software application or revision, replacement of systems or network hardware within your IT environment, etc.), and everything that must be accomplished to complete the work. The granularity of documenting these things – often referred to as levels in the WBS vernacular – will determine how you plan the next two constraints. Oh, and do not forget to add the management processes to the scope of your project:
  ◊ *Planning* at the beginning of the project.
  ◊ *Monitoring* work during the project.
  ◊ *Closing* the project at the end.

- **Time.** As part of planning, you analyze the things that need to be accomplished for the scope, determine the chronology for completing those things (including the management processes), and convert those things into *activities* (sometimes referred to as work packages) that will form your project's schedule. To determine how much time it will take to accomplish the project scope, you must consider two types of *time*:

- ◊ **Kairos Time.** For this type of time, you determine when the contributors are able to work on the project activities. I assume that you and your team have other duties to perform. How many hours each day will each person be able to dedicate to the project? You must factor in personal time off and other interruptions.

- ◊ **Chronos Time.** For this type of time, you forecast how many days, weeks, months, etc. it will take you and the team to complete all the project activities, depending on the results of your Kairos time analysis.

• **Cost.** For *de jure* projects, you would most likely have a budget. For *de facto* projects, you may not be given a budget to manage, but the project will incur costs, even if only the labor cost of you and the other contributors.

As part of planning – for both practice and proof – you forecast how many labor hours it will take over the entire schedule (Kairos time) to complete all the activities and achieve the project scope. If there are material costs as well, document those. The cost of these resources becomes your *de facto* budget. Remember to add the cost of the management processes referenced above.

Creating a Schedule

The most common tool used for creating a project schedule is the Gantt Chart. You do not need to grab a copy of the very expensive Microsoft Project application, or any other Gantt Chart software. But you do need to plan for and document the project schedule, the number of hours you forecast your team (or just you if you are the lone contributor) will spend on each project activity (Kairos time), and the absolute time you forecast your team will need to complete the project (Chronos time). A spreadsheet works fine. A pad and pencil would do. Technically, you could even use a calendar.

Microsoft Project and other Gantt Chart applications are also capable of monitoring a project budget. For a *de facto* project, I believe a spreadsheet application is more practical. Again, you can even use a pad of paper and a pencil.

Regardless of the medium you choose, you must plan for and document the total number of labor hours you forecast will be needed to complete the project (based on your Kairos time forecast). This forecast becomes your budget.

In the above paragraphs, I make the assumption that you control the time and cost elements of your project. You calculate, plan, and forecast both the schedule and the budget you believe is required to achieve the scope of the project. If your leadership gives you a deadline, and/or they limit the resources available to you for the project, you must reverse calculate the time and cost constraints to determine if you can successfully complete the project on their schedule and within their budget. If not, you will need to address this dilemma with your leadership.

Going through the above steps will help you build a convincing argument as to why the project is at risk unless they either reduce the scope, increase the time (delay the due date), and/or add more resources (cost).

Once you have documented the scope of your project, the full schedule (time), and the full cost of all the resources (labor hours plus any material), you then divide the scope into individual activities that you can monitor on a daily basis.

Daily would probably be excessive on larger, *de jure* projects, but it should be possible on smaller, *de facto* projects, and it makes the practice of monitoring the project easier. On whatever tool you decide to use – a project management application, a simple spreadsheet, or a pad of paper and pencil – document the individual activities you believe can be completed on each day of the schedule, and the number of hours each team member (or just you if you are a single contributor) must spend on those activities to complete them. By dividing the project into these individual activities, you should be able to determine the percentage of the project work you forecast will be completed each day.

With all this information documented, the planning processes of your project are complete, and it is time to execute.

Measuring Project Progress

The schedule will be the primary tool for managing the project once work begins, monitoring both time and cost on a daily basis. Did the team accomplish the project activities you forecasted for the day? Did they spend as many hours on the project as you had forecasted for the day? These two parameters reveal the daily status of the project based on time and cost as indicated below.

- **Project is on schedule and within budget if:**
  - ◊ The activities you forecasted were accomplished, and;
  - ◊ The team exerted the number of hours you forecasted.

- **Project is on schedule but over budget if:**
  - ◊ The activities you forecasted were accomplished, but;

◊ The team exerted more hours than you forecasted.

- **Project is behind schedule but within budget if:**
    ◊ The activities you forecasted were not accomplished, but;
    ◊ The team exerted fewer hours than you forecasted.

- **Project is behind schedule and over budget if:**
    ◊ The activities you forecasted were not accomplished, and;
    ◊ The team exerted more hours than you forecasted.

- **Project is ahead of schedule and within budget if:**
    ◊ More activities were accomplished than you forecasted, and;
    ◊ The team exerted the number of hours you forecasted.

- **Project is on schedule and under budget if:**
    ◊ The activities you forecasted were accomplished, and;
    ◊ The team exerted fewer hours than you forecasted.

- **Project is ahead of schedule and under budget if:**
    ◊ More activities were accomplished than you forecasted, and;
    ◊ The team exerted fewer hours than you forecasted.

By collecting this information, you would also be able to calculate the daily earned value of your project, but earned value management is beyond the intent of this chapter.

Learning from Your Projects

Eventually, when the project is complete and – hopefully – the scope has been achieved, you will be able to document if the project was completed on time and within the anticipated cost. If not, I assume your project was completed behind schedule and/or over budget. Do not despair.

The vast majority of projects – both *de facto* and *de jure* – do not match the forecast. The important thing is you make the effort to document the results, providing you proof of project management experience, and that you analyze why your project did not finish as expected.

Were there delays because team members were called off the project to do other things each day? Did certain activities take more effort or more time to accomplish than you anticipated? You take these lessons learned to do a better forecasting job next time. Practice leads to better performance – never to perfection.

In most cases, you need to account for resources (team members) not being available at the times you had hoped they would be, and to allot more days or weeks within the schedule than you otherwise would have. These are the first steps to implementing risk management.

And what about the results of the project? Did the deliverables meet the requirements? Were stakeholders satisfied with the results? If not, analyze the situation and document what could have been done better. These are the first steps to implementing quality management.

Risk and quality management are beyond the intent of this chapter, but analyzing what went wrong and determining how to proceed on future projects is practice, and the documentation provides proof.

Which covers the first two of the three P's. Now for the final P.

De Facto Projects and PMP Certification

The PMP is considered to be one of the most successful and respected certifications available. One reason is the extensive experience requirement that adds credibility to project managers who possess it.

Many aspiring candidates avoid registering for the certification examination because they doubt that they meet the experience requirement. I suggest that many of these candidates could prove their experience if they look back on previous years of their professional career, identify tasks that could have been transformed into *de facto* projects, and retroactively develop the documentation needed to prove project management experience.

Create a charter that includes the dates and duration of your projects, a brief description of the scope for those projects, your role (you may have been a contributor, but if you were not the person managing the project, do not include that particular *de facto* project), a summary of the resultant deliverable(s), the number of team members (if you were the only contributor, do not include that *de facto* project either), and the budget (which could simply be the estimated cost of the labor hours for you and the entire team).

Now, before you submit these examples of projects you have managed, show the charter to whomever was your supervisor during the project, and solicit their approval. This step is important, because PMI audits a certain number of PMP submissions each year. If that occurs for your submission, you will need to ask those supervisors to fill out and sign a form from PMI confirming you performed the work being claimed. By proactively alerting these individuals and getting their approval in advance, you will not be worried by the possibility of the dreaded audit.

Check with PMI for the exact work experience required as the details change from time to time.

If you feel there are not enough suitable tasks in your past that could be transformed into *de facto* projects that a supervisor would sign to meet PMI's requirements, then begin today! Follow the advice I have provided on transforming tasks into *de facto* projects, and before you know it, you will have what it takes to apply for the PMP.

CHAPTER SIX

Good Communication Practices Throughout the Project Lifecycle

By Walt Sparling

In the real estate world, an agent's mantra is "location, location, location." This is because with all things being equal, location is the one key factor that can and will determine ultimate success in a real estate venture. In the project management world, it is all about "communication, communication, communication," and like the real estate world, all other things being equal, the project with the best communication will come out on top.

All project managers seasoned or new learn as they go, and levels of communication will increase the larger and more complex projects get. If you are just starting out, understand that communication will be an important skill to master and make sure you spend a fair amount of learning and skill development on this key skill.

I would bet that most experienced people would not argue

on either the location or communication aspects of each respective industry, but how do we make sure that we follow the respective mantras? I am not a real estate person and although I have many friends that are, I can speak little to their industry. Project management, on the other hand, is what I do and have done for many years. Let's talk about communication and why it is so important.

Communication in All Its Forms

To get things started, I am going to cover the various forms of communication, then dive into the ways that each method can be used on a project to help make it successful.

Communication happens through a variety of methods, with each having levels of success depending on how they are implemented. As we know it, communication most commonly happens via one of three ways; verbal, written and visual. Each one of these has multiple subsets and often a combination of one or more is used to communicate an idea, concept, or concern.

One of the oldest and most common forms is verbal communication. Verbal communication is often done through face-to-face interactions, telephone or video calls, or voice messages. Verbal communication happens in meetings, presentations, video and voice recordings, and basic one-on-one conversations. Way before the current world of technology tools, verbal communication was the best way to convey a point, concern, or idea.

When doing verbal communication in-person or through video, one on one or in a group, you also need to understand the importance of body language. Do you appear comfortable and confident, do you portray a lack of interest, or maybe even distrust? This is probably one of the hardest skills to master as people will read you based on their personal thoughts or experiences on what your body language means to them. Body language is an art and I encourage you to spend time on this to hone your skills. This skill could be a chapter in itself, so I encourage you to research this topic to help you up your game for in-person and video communications.

Written communication is the best way to share very detailed information, as having someone go on and on about legal or statistical information can and will often be mind-numbing. Written communication is also the most common way to archive and save information that requires a historical record, while providing the ability to share and review a communication at a time that is more convenient to an audience.

Visual communication is something that can be done as a stand-alone product or one that is included or added to other methods to successfully get a point across or share information. Visual communication is often done through pictures, diagrams, or videos.

In our modern world, visual communication has taken on a much more prominent role. As an example, consider the more common everyday tasks of portraying emotions or thoughts to friends, family and even business associates using emoticons in texts and emails. You need to be careful though on using emoticons, as some may interpret them differently than your intention. Simple symbols can convey emotions or opinions that most people will associate with a communication of ideas or feelings.

When thinking visually, think of the common phrase that "A picture is worth a thousand words". Pictures or videos used to show progress or snapshots of dashboards can quickly communicate progress on your projects.

A common type of communication method, especially since the COVID-19 pandemic, is virtual meetings. Virtual meetings can be conducted via Zoom, Microsoft Teams, Skype, or a variety of other technologies. These meetings should be treated as in-person meetings. These types of meetings can be tough for some, as many attendees may not want to be on video.

As the project manager, you need to set expectations for virtual meetings. Although you cannot force attendees to be on video, you can encourage it. Not having people on video loses the in-person cues, body language, and facial expressions that provide feedback that you need to interpret communication. As the project manager, you can encourage, but cannot control. Be willing to adapt and overcome.

A successful project manager will use all the above communication methods at various stages of their project to share data, convey importance and keep the project team up to date.

Verbal communications will be used in individual phone calls, conference calls, and one-on-one conversations. Written communications will be used to convey contract requirements, specifications, and document historical data. Visual communications will be used to clearly define objectives, and show historical information through graphs, charts, and photographs.

Accountability, Communication, and Project Success

As a project manager, how you use the various methods of communication available to you can make a huge difference in the success of your project. The important thing here is to know your audience. All projects have various parties involved (stakeholders) that you need to communicate with. Knowing the needs of your audience will help determine your communication methods.

Projects have varying levels of complexity and with that comes varying communication requirements. In a more formal project management structure, there are methods to track what specific people need to know, when they need to know it and how the information will be conveyed to them.

In my world of multi-million-dollar projects with many people involved, I must have a method of determining how to communicate with each of them. But in any project of any size this remains a critical consideration.

Projects have stakeholders, a broad term that includes anyone that is directly involved in or is affected by your project. Stakeholders will vary by your industry, and may include developers, programmers, design partners, contractors, customers, and end-users. All these individuals require specific levels of communication.

RACI: Monitoring Communication at Varying Levels

A simple way to determine how communication is handled is through what is called a RACI matrix. RACI is a simple concept that can be applied to projects of any size and will help anyone develop a basis for a communication plan.

RACI is an acronym that stands for *Responsible, Accountable, Consulted,* and *Informed.* This boils down to the notion that certain people on a project have responsible roles, some are held accountable for specific outcomes in the project, some need to be consulted on the steps and some just need to be informed about what is happening.

By knowing the roles of people on your project, you can determine the communication methods used to "communicate" with them.

Responsible and accountable roles are significant and will typically be one of the areas where *your* role as a project manager is covered. As a project manager, you are likely going to be ultimately "responsible" for the project's success. You may report to people that are accountable to a higher authority, which could affect your ability to perform your role. These individuals may require a high level of communication via a combination of verbal, written and visual presentations.

Accountable stakeholders are those that you often need to communicate with verbally and in writing to make sure that they are aware of what is happening and to get approvals from when required. These are the people that are ultimately at risk if the project fails.

The stakeholders that you "Consult" with are also important, as they provide information to you that you share with others on the team to complete one or more tasks of the project. The consultant stakeholders are often referred to as SMEs (Subject Matter Experts). This is an area where verbal, written and visual communications are key. You need to communicate the consultant's information or requirements to all the other stakeholders.

The "informed" stakeholders are those that you need to keep "in the know." These stakeholders need to know what is happening overall, but do not necessarily need to know every detail. This is a great opportunity to provide minimal written and visual communications to provide a summary of what the project status is. An executive summary or BLUF (Bottom Line Up front), and some pictures or graphs may be all you need to keep them up to date.

In any project, you will have "key" stakeholders. Many of these are high-level executives or your project sponsor, and it is your job to keep them informed, but they may also need to weigh in on key decisions. Understand that these individu-

Good Communication Practices   97

RACI Matrix			PROJECT PHASES																		
			Initiation		Planning									Execution							
R	RESPONSIBLE Person(s) responsible for completing assigned deliverables		Project Proposal-Submission Form	Sizing Matrix	Initiation Business Case	Kickoff	SharePoint Site Set up	Project Charter	RISK Management Workbook	Marketing Brief (Marketing Projects)	Request for information (RFI)	Business Requirements	Request for Proposal (RFP)	Deliverables Matrix	Communication Plan	Marketing Plan	Project Management Plan	Vendor Design Document (Vendor)	IT Network & Systems Diagrams	IT Tech Specifications	IT Operational Guide	Business Continuity Plan	Policies and Procedures	Vendor Statement of Work	Project Schedule through Completion	Install Hardware AND Software	Training Plan	Execute Communication Plan
A	ACCOUNTABLE Ultimate Owner, Accountable for final decision																											
C	CONSULTED Person consulted before performing an action or a decision is made																											
I	INFORMED Person informed after action or decision - Keep in the know																											
	Project Participants																											
Project Sponsor			A	A	I	I		I	I								I					I		I	I	I		
Business Owner			R	R	R	A	C	A	A	I	A	A	A	A	I	I				I	I	R	A	C	A	I	A	A
Main Project Manager				I		R	R	R	R	I	C	C	C	R	R	A	A	I	I	I	I	C	I	A	R	I	I	I
IT Project Manager						C	I	C	C		C	I	C	I	I			A	A	I	I		I	R	R	I	I	
Architect						I	I	I	I	C		C	I	C	I	I			I	I	R	R		I	C	R		I
Technical Writer																							R					
Project Reviewer				I		I	I	I	I			I	I	I	I			I	I				I	I	I			
Engineer				I		I	I	I	C			I	I						I	I	I			I	C	I		I

This is an example of what a RACI Matrix looks like. Not all processes may apply or be set up the same for each project or organization.

als may be overseeing multiple projects and are very busy. To respect their schedule yet make sure that they are knowledgeable about what is happening on the project, you need to give them a brief summary. This is typically an intro paragraph in your status updates of the overall project status and possibly action items or decisions that you need to keep the project moving, this is where the executive summary of BLUF come in.

The point of the executive summary or BLUF is to provide sufficient information for them to be knowledgeable about what is happening without having to read all the details of your update. They can read further into your update or reach out to you for more detailed information – it is about respecting their time.

Optimizing Verbal Communication

Once you have figured out your audience and what needs to be provided, you need to figure out how to optimize those communications. This is where things get fun. Let's talk about verbal communications. One of my favorite quotes by George Bernard Shaw is:

"The single biggest problem in communication is the illusion that it has taken place."

How many conversations have you had with individuals or a group that you feel that you made your point and that you both or all involved were on the same understanding about the point or topic, only to find out later that it was not the case?

Verbal communications can be tricky, as they are often conducted in a private one on one setting or phone call and the others in the conversation may be distracted and not fully engaged.

With verbal communications, a best practice is to do a follow-up in writing about the conversation to make sure the agreed-upon understanding is accurate. A quick way to validate this is to send a written correspondence (typically an email) to all those involved stating your understanding about the conversation and that unless you hear otherwise, you will proceed with those facts. Give the parties a reasonable but specific timeframe to reply to the contrary or acceptance before you move ahead. If timing is critical, follow-up with a phone call.

When having verbal communications, a key skill is "active listening." Conversations are meant to be a two-way street, otherwise it would just be you "talking" and hoping that the other party or parties are truly engaged and are understanding what has been communicated. I recommend that you research the term "active listening" online and learn more about what it means, but a few key points are listed below. First avoid evaluative listening:

- Hold off forming opinions until the speaker's message is complete.

- Don't obsess with or focus on emotional words or phrases.

- Concentrate on the speaker, not on an intended rebuttal.

- There are several steps to take to ensure active listening:

- Truly listen by providing the speaker with your undivided attention.

- Reduce or eliminate noise or other distractions.

- Organize the message you hear.

- Check your understanding of what's been said by repeating it back in your own words.

Optimizing Written Communication

Written communication is a great tool for documenting statuses and requirements. Written communication can be used to validate an understanding from verbal communication. When it comes to conveying very detailed information or requirements, written communication is typically the best way to do so.

Written communication can be shared with many stakeholders at once, it can be used as a historical means of tracking conversations, and it can be used to spell out levels of detail that are not easy to do with a verbal conversation alone.

Examples of written communication in the realm of project management include daily correspondence through emails, meeting minutes, status updates, questionnaires, specifications, process steps, task lists, etc. Written communications can also involve tweets and texts, although these are not commonly used as means for business communication as many are generational based. Remember – know your audience.

Knowing your audience helps in how to format and share your written communications. Because written communication has such a broad range of options, you need to consider the points that need to be made and how succinct or detailed you need to make them.

When spelling out specifications or project requirements, detail is important, but when providing status updates, brevity is the way to go. For specifications and specific requirements, you want to make the communication as detailed as possible, which could involve pages of information to make sure all objectives are covered. When sharing status updates, you need to make sure that key points are communicated but avoid excess information that could cause distractions or confusion for your audience. This is where an executive summary or BLUF provides the best level of detail.

An executive summary or BLUF is a short document or paragraph that is provided, typically for, as the statement indicates – executives or *key* stakeholders. As was stated previously, in the business world, executives are extremely busy, and their time is limited. You need to communicate your idea or update in a manner that gets your points across in a brief yet clear way. The readers need to be able to quickly become acquainted with the facts about something that may be pulled from a much larger body of material without them having to read it all.

This summary will often include key project information, like the status of schedule milestones and budget adherence as well as action items. To do this successfully, you may need to combine your written summary with the last form of communication – visual.

Optimizing Visual Communication

Visual is the third type of communication and one that can provide a lot of detail in the form of graphs, diagrams, charts, and pictures. Visual representations of a schedule, a budget snapshot via a screenshot from accounting software, and photos of the current progress of an ongoing project, are all very useful methods to communicate ideas and project status.

In the modern world of communication, PowerPoint is a very common way of presenting data to an audience of all sizes. Figuring out how to best present the data through PowerPoint or some other similar tool is a skill. Be creative, but keep your audience in mind. PowerPoint is a visual communication tool – don't just fill slides with text.

Over the course of a project, a project manager needs to keep all stakeholders up-to-date with a myriad of information. This information will include the project schedule, budget, risks, resources, and lessons learned. It is not uncommon for companies to have a standard format for status updates that are geared to a specific audience, so multiple formats may be required.

To keep your project moving ahead, get the approvals and buy-in that you need to make it successful, you need to know the various forms of communications that are at your disposal and how to best use them. To master the three forms of communication, I encourage you to study, read, and follow the examples of other successful project managers so that you can master your trade and ultimately be a successful project manager yourself.

The Basics of Email: Small Steps with Big Payoffs

With the three common methods of communication outlined, let's dive into some specifics that modern project managers will deal with, with the most prevalent being email.

Email communication is the life blood of the modern world when it comes to communicating with stakeholders. Texting and live streaming are other methods that are making significant headway into modern communication methods, but I will touch on those a bit later.

Email has its strengths and weaknesses and if you want to master it, you need to understand some key aspects.

As I have stated earlier – knowing your audience is key.

Not all stakeholders are up on the use of email, and some will downright hate it, but it is an important part of communicating information and in my mind will be for some time.

An aspect of email that many do not get is basic email etiquette. You cannot expect all stakeholders to get it, but you as the project manager need to follow some basic etiquette rules to avoid communication failures.

Let's start with a basic definition of "etiquette." The online Business dictionary defines business etiquette as:

> "Expected behaviors and expectations for individual actions within society, group, or class. Within a place of business, it involves treating coworkers and employers with respect and courtesy in a way that creates a pleasant work environment for everyone."

So, for email, my translation would be the "expected behavior that involves treating coworkers, clients, your employer and friends with respect and courtesy when sending email."

In office environments people are often sending or receiving emails to communicate needs, requirements, and schedules and it is used to share documents with stakeholders.

The key to understanding email is that it is a form of written communication and although not verbal, it requires some of the same basic principles of being clear and concise. In many cases, email communication needs even more thought because you do not have the advantage of the non-verbal body language cues you get with face-to-face communication.

Email Basics for Successful Stakeholder Engagement

Addressing. When addressing email recipients, be clear on who it is going to and who needs to be copied. There are three typical lines that can be used in an email correspondence, if you do not have these options, either your email program is very limited, or they are turned off – typically the later. These three addressing options are "TO", "CC", and "BCC".

> **TO.** This is for who the email is primarily "addressed to." This can be more than one person, but it is typically only a few people. Typically, you would be addressing an individual or as said before a few people and then copying others to make sure they are "In the loop."

> Commonly accepted practice is that anyone on the "TO" line is being directly addressed and comments or questions are being directed to them and they should respond. This is important if you start asking questions or making comments that need answers. If the email was addressed to everyone directly it could be understood that everyone needs to respond. The problem comes in when all these people do respond.

CC. (Carbon Copy – as in old school carbon paper). This line is used to copy other individuals that are not necessarily being directly addressed but need ot be in the know.

Commonly accepted practice is that anyone on the "CC" line is being copied for courtesy or information use, as in informing stakeholders, so that they know what is happening, what issues are being addressed, etc. but their response is not necessarily required. If you are "CC'd" but you are specifically addressed in the body of the email itself, then that changes things, and you should respond or act accordingly.

BCC. This is used to privately copy recipients like your manager for their reference or information and should be used sparingly in the professional world.

Subject line. What is this email about? Blank subject lines are annoying – did the sender (i.e., *you*) not know what the email was about? Emails are not texts – they have a subject. Efficient users use the subject line for sorting, searching, and filing. Users that do not have a preview pane showing up will get nothing under the subject line. Should they open it? Is it a real email? Although this is annoying on a personal email basis, it is seen as unprofessional and will often be flagged as spam or junk mail.

Importance. If you select the "important" option for all your emails, which unfortunately a lot of people tend to do, it is a lot like crying wolf. Don't get me wrong, I look at these on an individual basis, and if it is a new person or someone who rarely uses it, I will look at it right away. Otherwise, it will wait in line just like the rest of the non-important emails.

Presentation, grammar, and punctuation. How many

times does someone need to read an email to get what it means? This does not really take a lot of effort, just start by using periods and commas. It's not important that you use commas and periods appropriately.

If you are sending email as part of your work/business, please use spell check. An occasional misspelling is understandable, but consistent spelling mistakes and horrible grammar in an email is just unacceptable in today's world. In Outlook and Gmail, spelling and grammar checking is an automatic feature – just turn it on and leave it. Consider a third-party application like Grammarly to keep your emails professional.

Signature. Who are you, and how do I contact you if I have questions – other than a reply? How about a name, company, and phone number as a minimum? Signatures are very easy to set up in most common email applications. Not providing some basic signature information can cause a lot of extra work on the recipient to get back to you – especially if you are not someone that they typically communicate with.

Reply all. If you are on the "TO" line and sometimes on the "CC" line, you may wish to or even be asked to reply. When this happens, do a "reply all" so that everyone has the benefit of your response. The others may need to hear what you have to say and that is why they are "CCd."

Thank you replies do NOT need to be a "Reply all" – it just adds frivolous emails to people's inbox.

Email Key Takeaways

- When addressing email recipients in business, be clear on who it is going to "TO:" and who needs to be copied "CC:."

- Include a subject.

- Do *not* indicate *all* your emails as "Important;" the more you do it, the less important your emails become.

- Spell and grammar check your emails.

- Indicate more in your signature than your first name.

Summary

Communication as a project manager is a key skill for project success. There are a variety of communication methods, and you need to be familiar with each one and know when to implement them on your project based on your audience.

When having verbal or in-person communications, follow up with a summary of your understanding and be cognizant of your body language.

When creating written communications, consider the use of an executive summary or BLUF and utilize a spelling and grammar checking tool.

When communicating visually, provide relevant and quality graphics and don't overload your presentations with a lot of text.

Above all, no matter the communication method used, know your audience and provide communications that will make the most impact for them.

Resources for Additional Communication Learning

- *Crucial Conversations: Tools for Talking When Stakes Are High,* by Kerry Patterson, Joseph Greeny, Tron McMillan, Al Switzler and Laura Rope.

- *We Need to Talk: How to Have Conversations That Matter,* by Celeste Headlee.

- *The 16 Undeniable Laws of Communication,* by John Maxwell.

- *A Guide to the Project Management Body of Knowledge (PMBOK Guide), Sixth Edition,* Project Management Institute.

CHAPTER SEVEN

From Manager to Leader: Unboxing the Power of Value-Based Performance and Personal Branding

By Tareka Wheeler

In the dynamic landscape of project management, success isn't just about delivering on time and within budget anymore. In the era of constant change and innovation, project managers need to shift their focus towards value-based performance. This involves not only meeting project objectives but also ensuring that every effort contributes to the overarching strategic goals of the organization.

In tandem with this, establishing and articulating a personal brand is crucial for project managers aiming to thrive in their roles and advance in their careers. Believe it or not, this reminds me of Christmas.

Value is the gift that keeps on giving. I absolutely love Christmas. As a child, my brother and I were serious about Christmas, and made sure that my mom knew we were deserving of all that Santa was planning to bring us. Picture this: it was Christmas morning, and the excitement radiated from my brother and I as we rushed into the living room to find a ton of wrapped presents under the tree. Each box held the promise of something new and exciting.

My brother and I tore into the first box with eager anticipation, and my eyes lit up as I discovered a Light Bright. "Imagine the possibilities!" My imagination was running wild about all the pictures and patterns I was going to create for everyone to see. Each gift brought a unique blend of excitement and potential as always and Santa never seemed to disappoint.

In the same way, project managers can find themselves with a collection of unique gifts and talents. Just like our presents, these skills are waiting to be unwrapped and utilized to create something extraordinary.

Project managers have many gifts within themselves. It's important that you tap into acknowledging, unwrapping, and embracing these talents so you can elevate your performance and make your mark as a leader in this invaluable discipline and field. Each project leader has a unique combination of skills waiting to be unboxed. By authentically embracing these gifts, project managers can create a bold brand that sets them apart as high-performing leaders in the world of project management.

It's About Value

As you aspire to be a high performing project manager, I want to challenge you to shift from being a project manager to a project leader. This shift requires you to embrace the importance of not just doing a good job with traditional project delivery. You must tap into "value-based performance."

Value-based performance begins with a deep understanding of organizational or project goals. Project leaders must align their projects with the broader strategy, ensuring that every task contributes to the overall success of the company. It's important to regularly reassess project goals in the context of the organization's evolving needs and adjust strategies accordingly.

As a project leader, you simply can't get stuck in your own ways and thinking. Honestly, your performance is not about you. Your performance is about the value that you bring to all the stakeholders involved in your project. I believe in stakeholder centric leadership. Value, in this context, is not just about completing tasks; it's about delivering outcomes that enhance the bottom line and overall stakeholder satisfaction.

The big question you might be asking is "what can I do to shift into value-based performance"? Here are some practical strategies you can use as a project leader.

- **Discover and define value.** Communicate with key stakeholders to gain a clear understanding of what is desired and needed beyond standard project delivery. What can you provide or deliver that has long-term or sustainable value?

- **Define clear objectives.** Clearly articulate project objectives aligned with organizational strategy. Ensure that team members understand the broader context of their tasks and how they contribute to the overall value.

- **Conduct continuous evaluation and adaptation.** Regularly assess project progress and adjust strategies as needed. Agile methodologies can be particularly useful in this regard, allowing for flexibility and quick adaptations to changing requirements.

- **Actively manage potential risks.** Anticipate and mitigate risks that could hinder the delivery of value. Being proactive in risk management ensures that unexpected challenges don't derail the project's overall success.

- **Measure Key Performance Indicators (KPIs):** Develop and track KPIs that align with project and organizational goals. Use these metrics not only for project monitoring but also for demonstrating the value generated to stakeholders.

Building Your Project Leader Brand

Now that you have shifted to value-based performance, it's important to be mindful of how you show up! Building and articulating your brand as a project leader is critical. Establishing a personal brand as a project leader is not about self-promotion, but about showcasing your unique value proposition.

In project management, where each task demands precision and strategic thinking, the concept of personal branding may seem like an extraneous layer. However, as we dig into the intricacies of leadership, it becomes evident that your professional narrative is not just a luxury but a necessity - a key that unlocks doors to success in the world of project leadership.

Imagine a scenario where your name isn't just associated with the tasks you accomplish but resonates as a symbol of competence, reliability, and value. Your personal brand is the amplifier that increases your visibility within your organization and the broader industry. As your stakeholders and colleagues get to know your brand, you go beyond the limits of your projects and become the person everyone turns to for important initiatives and insights.

Over my 20 years in project and program management, I have not always understood the importance of personal branding. It wasn't until the middle of my career when I got a

Value-Based Performance and Personal Branding

big wake up call.

I was always working hard, doing all that was asked of me and then some. Yes, I was not progressing or advancing in my career. Everyone knew I was good at my job; however, they did not know about my full potential that I was keeping boxed up where nobody could see them. I found myself being appreciated but not promoted. I decided that had to change.

I decided that I was going to show up for me and start articulating and demonstrating my value and ultimately my brand. I wanted to drive the narrative of my professional reputation so that management and senior leaders would not only appreciate my hard work but would see and value all that I was bringing to the table.

Once I made that pivot, I never turned back. Now, I can confidently say and consistently demonstrate that "I am a dynamic project leader known for orchestrating seamless collaborations and delivering results that align with organizational objectives. With a keen eye for detail and a knack for strategic problem-solving, I transform project challenges into opportunities."

Think about your personal brand. Can you articulate what you leave behind? Are you confident in the impressions you are making and what your reputation is perceived to be? If you're not quite sure, let's explore how you can build, enhance, or repair your personal brand as a project leader.

- **Identify your strengths.** Understand your strengths and unique skills that set you apart from others. Arc you exceptionally skilled in risk management, stakeholder communication, or problem-solving? Identify these key strengths write them down and be intentional about how you use them.

- **Consistent communication.** Articulate your achievements clearly and consistently. Regularly communicate not just project successes but also the challenges you've overcome, and the lessons learned. Do this is project meetings, reports, and one-on-one interactions with leadership and key stakeholders.

- **Networking.** Actively engage with peers, superiors, and industry professionals. Networking helps in building a reputation beyond the confines of your current project or organization.

- **Constantly show up and show out.** How can they know who you are if you don't show them. As a project leader, you must break out of the box and constantly show up for yourself. Identify opportunities to demonstrate value. Accept opportunities to lead or support highly visible projects or initiatives and execute them in your unique way.

Going the Extra Mile

The bottom line is that you must show up beyond what is expected of you. Solid project delivery is expected. Make the shift from being a project manager to a project leader by delivering value and articulating your personal brand.

A well-defined personal brand opens up opportunities for career advancement and enhances your leadership impact. Team members are more likely to follow and trust a leader with a clear and positive reputation, and employers are more likely to retain and invest in individuals who are recognized for their unique contributions.

Value-based performance and personal branding are interconnected elements that elevate project managers from task executors to project leaders. Embrace these principles and strategies and watch as your projects become not just tasks on a timeline but integral components to achieving the professional success you desire and deserve.

CHAPTER EIGHT

Lessons from Outside: Infinite Diversity in Infinite Combinations

By John Connolly

It's more difficult than it initially might appear to distill advice and guidance for other project managers on their path through their careers. Not only are there many themes and topics to choose from, but it borders on overwhelming to make advice applicable to the many circumstances project managers typically find themselves.

With this in mind, I decided to put forward my thoughts on how project managers are often made, drawing on my own story.

Stories, I believe, are extremely powerful because they reflect the heart of how human beings learn about each other and the world around them. In that vein, I returned to a fictitious realm to inform and develop a framing of my true-to-life story.

An Influx of Diverse Talent

Astute consumers of the Star Trek franchise may readily recognize the title of this chapter. "Infinite Diversity in Infinite Combinations" is the foundational principle of philosophy for the Vulcan species.

The philosophy is founded on the concept that beauty, growth, and progress stem from the combination of the *unlike* far more than the *alike*. So too with project management. I believe the concept is easily applicable to what makes project management strong, and how we can focus our path forward for the project management field.

Over the course of the past several years, project management has risen quickly in recognition as a discipline. PMI has identified demand for 25 million new project roles by 2030, making it a good time to deepen the profession's reach and recruitment. As of this writing, 1.4 million project managers hold their PMP certification from PMI, a figure that I expect to grow in the future.

I have noted a dramatic increase in employers advertising open roles requiring project experience. When I first began noticing open roles, they were listed as "PMP or CAPM certification desired." Now, many of the same sorts of roles are listed as "PMP or CAPM certification required."

At the same time as the recognition of the field has grown, a rising tide of professionals are pivoting careers into project management. It's difficult to evaluate these transitioning professionals as a trend, as every circumstance is different. As a profession, I think it's incumbent on established project managers to help these professionals thread the needle on entry into the field. These newer project professionals will require guidance, mentorship, training, and in many circumstances, certification to give them the tools to succeed in project management.

On the other side of the coin, these professionals will need to commit to learning and applying project management tools and approaches to build experience.

Combining the Unlike to Form Strength

In this context, it's important that established project managers and newcomers to the field both understand and value the infinite diversity that can be realized for our profession if we embrace infinite combinations. That begins with the recognition and appreciation of the background and experience that new professionals bring to project management.

Candidates making a career transition are often advised to drop their "irrelevant" experience from their resumes, opting to focus exclusively on "transferrable" skills and experience. In my experience, this is usually shorthand for a focus entirely on the skills that readily fit into the established project management box that most employers and project managers think of when it comes to the skillsets of a project manager.

I once discussed this very issue with a candidate looking to make a shift in her career. She had been advised to drop off vast swaths of her professional experience in order to cover up "irrelevant" career activities. This person had founded their own business, managed at a senior directorship level, and had also worked in education. I advised her to embrace her strengths, especially her leadership abilities. The fixation on areas of technical expertise were obscuring the fact that this person had managed dozens of senior managers for a large organization. The advice to cut her career in half on paper missed the mark.

Where is the mark, then? In my opinion, it's to be found in opening the door of project management wider, admitting and building up professionals who bring a vast variety of backgrounds and experiences to the field. There are thousands of project professionals in industries that are not typically considered for their project work and yet nevertheless have a heavy emphasis on project work.

Unlikely Backgrounds and Unconsidered Experience

My background is in libraries and information management. I got my start in that industry as a teenager, working in the cataloging department of my college's academic library. Over the years, I worked with metadata and database management, software implementation and training, and eventually moved into a management role for a small library and art museum before moving into a role at a larger public library.

Libraries are awash in projects, and nobody (inside or outside the library field) is any the wiser to this fact. Looking back, I am amazed at the number of projects that are initiated, planned, executed, monitored, and closed by librarians of all kinds. In fact, I think that formal project management tools would be a deeply valuable asset to the library field, since so many projects are undertaken so frequently.

And yet, it's imperative to resist the myopic tendency to focus on this fact as if it's a one-way street. Having made the transition from "a librarian who manages projects" to "a project manager with a library background," I believe librarians have invaluable lessons to teach project managers, too. In one of my library roles, I managed a team of librarians who collectively had more project experience than a great many project managers I've encountered in other industries.

One of my best project manager librarians had been in her

role at the library for a very long time. She was tireless in her planning and execution of educational events and strategic partnerships with other organizations. As the library had shifted its focus during the COVID-19 pandemic, this librarian was under-utilized. I firmly believe her manager had mistakenly moved her out of a role that leveraged her project management skills and had forced her into a technical subject matter expert (SME) role that didn't suit her well.

The moment I stepped into my leadership role on her team, this librarian knocked on my door to say, "I can do more than I'm being asked to do." I immediately promised there would be plenty of work.

As we reopened services after a lengthy pandemic closure, I delivered on my promise. I pulled her back from an SME role and threw as many projects at her as I could. The planning and execution of educational events of all kinds, including creative programming on a threadbare (or nonexistent) budget, came to life rapidly.

This librarian, who had been in her role as a community servant for decades, leveraged her connections like no other. She made excellent use of her skills to communicate with others and an outstanding political awareness to bring resources in from outside our organization. Before I knew it, we were hosting live bands, leading language education events, and hosting free concerts that filled an auditorium with hundreds of attendees on Sunday afternoons.

Through it all, I did little more than watch and learn. The lessons I gleaned have been beneficial to me to this day. And I wonder how many expert project managers in libraries have missed their chance to contribute their knowledge and experience to other realms of project management simply because neither librarians nor project managers really think of each other as related disciplines.

Preparing for Change and Opportunity for Learning

The missed opportunities for learning represent a massive weakness for project management. As long as project managers consider themselves to be a source of knowledge instead of a community of learners, we will continue to miss the lessons afforded to us by so many project managers in under-appreciated professions.

A great many newcomers to the project management field are coming out of healthcare or education, two fields that go deeply under-appreciated in our society. And yet, these professionals are highly educated, extraordinarily motivated, and hold vast experience in meticulously executing projects with demanding scope and little to no budget and resources.

I tell people outside of the project field that project management isn't an industry, it's a discipline that can be applied to many different industries. I'm certain that the execution of projects in education, healthcare, non-profits, and many other industries have generated new knowledge about good practices for project management. These lessons have gone unlearned because we haven't discovered the commonality between easily recognizable project management roles and those managing "non-traditional" projects.

The wonderful news, however, is that these lessons are now being brought to us. Newcomers to project management have begun to flow into our online groups, our PMI chapters, and our job applicant platforms. Each of these professionals represents lessons for our field that will shape our path forward. New techniques and insights are walking in the doors to the project management field. The most pressing question isn't how *we* are going to change them to make them like us. The urgent question is how will we harness the knowledge from *them.* **Are we paying attention to their lessons learned?**

Experience is Greater than Theory – Even Outside of Traditional Project Roles

When I first started managing projects, I had zero experience or guidance to assist me. I did not have the tools and frameworks that are common throughout the project management field to assist me. I was unaware that PMI existed, much less that it might have vital tools to help me manage my projects.

My first exposure to project work was a "trial by fire" in a functional environment where I didn't have a full-time team under me. While that changed over time, I had to learn early how to negotiate and convince, rather than direct and correct.

I stepped into a new role as a librarian and was immediately awash in projects. The organization was suffering from deeply outdated tools and workflows, greatly hindering the mission of the library and the ability of researchers to find and use the collection. Boxes upon boxes of donated archival materials were stacked up in the basement, awaiting sorting and cataloging. Rare books in need of repairs were piled up in odd corners. And the librarian's role was integral to arranging and hosting several fancy donor events each year, each event requiring management of its own scope, schedule, and cost.

As I taught myself the ropes through trial and error, I learned many things. I learned about budgeting and accounting, generating profit and loss reports, and building out comprehensive, intelligible project reports for the library's steering committee and Board of Directors.

I learned to navigate fraught political environments with high-powered donors and stakeholders, some of whom didn't approve of changes I made to the library through these projects. I also learned to coordinate tasks and activities for multiple deliverables with interconnected workstreams using a variety of predictive and Agile tools, the only experience I had in my background from working in a software company.

I didn't learn any of this alone. I had supportive colleagues and willing help from the part-time and volunteer teams doing the project's work. But more than all this, I was working for a gifted and visionary leader who recognized my abilities early and guided me on my journey to leadership and successful project completion.

My broad point is that I gathered a wealth of knowledge and applied it with success to my projects. When I finally discovered PMI and the PMP certification (almost ten years after beginning to manage projects), I was astonished at the tools available to project managers. I was also surprised how many things I was already doing that I simply didn't have a vocabulary to describe. Project management as a discipline gave me that vocabulary and opened new avenues of exploration to me.

It is precisely at this point that additional care and attention must be given for a successful transition from managing projects into being a project manager. I consider mentorship and education in project management's well-established tools and practices to be essential. However, I would give a word of caution to newcomers to the field as well. Don't abandon what has brought you so far. Instead, attempt to serve the field by connecting the dots and finding your special expertise. Project management needs a diversity of voices and lessons now more than ever.

Building Structures for Bidirectional Exchange of Knowledge

Very few workers are coming to project management as a blank slate, ready to have a complete set of tools loaded into their brains. In fact, a great many project managers with whom I've spoken have a similar shape to their journey to project management as I had. They were approached by a manager and tasked with a project to complete. These projects often are executed in deeply functional environments, with little or no budget, but with exacting deliverables and deadlines.

The newborn project manager must teach themselves how to accomplish the tasks needed, experiencing a "baptism by fire" similar to my own. Having proven their ability by successful navigation of the crucible of their first project, they are then given more projects to complete. After repeating this cycle, eventually the project manager learns about the tools in formal project management, leveraging their experience and often getting certified before moving into a formal project manager role.

I perceive an increase in these nascent project managers following this arc out of a previous line of work. They are often at a loss of what to do and where to go. Many gravitate toward PMI and its chapters, with mixed success in finding mentorship and guidance. They need assistance clarifying their career goals and understanding how to apply their deep experience in a foreign set of frameworks and terminology.

To project managers who are already established in the field, I strongly suggest that the burden falls on our shoulders to both teach and learn from newcomers in equal measure. In my experience, I find that much of the involvement in this activity is unfairly assumed to be the role of PMI and its chapters. And while this is a legitimate function for PMI to a limited extent, I haven't seen deliberate, structured approaches to leverage new knowledge as a priority.

PMI does consider itself a global Community of Practice, but it also assumes the burden of setting standards, offering credentials and certifications, and promoting thought leadership across the project management field. It's unlikely that such a large organization will alone suffice for all purposes.

In the end, I believe that nothing will beat the organic interplay of new knowledge entering the field with the insights of seasoned project veterans. I think the project managers who are most committed to facilitating this knowledge transfer will reap significant benefits from assuming roles as mentors and connectors.

By connection, I'm not referring to networking to support career growth, although that is still something that can be facilitated for newcomers into the field. Rather, I mean that connection between concepts and application of ideas should be a high priority when welcoming newcomers into project management. The better we are at understanding where we can learn, the clearer we shall be on how new ideas can be applied.

The Responsibility to Teach and to Learn

Established project managers are experts. They have an excellent view from 10,000 feet, orchestrating and coordinating action to harmonize projects and bring them to successful conclusions. That knowledge and expertise is an invaluable resource to the project management field, and it needs to be transferred to newcomers as efficiently and quickly as is practical. However, established project managers are also uniquely positioned to guide newcomers in the successful application of their pre-existing skills and experience into project work.

The rise of ad-hoc, organic communities of project managers in online venues has been gratifying to see over the past few years. These groups allow for relationships to build via word-of-mouth and digital interactions. As relationships deepen, colleagues learn from one another's unique insights and ideas. These environments are where true, long-term mentorships can thrive to the benefit of all involved. There is, however, much more work to be done.

There have never been more eyes on project management than now. Project managers are being observed with intense interest by those who are considering entering formal project management or who have already decided to make the leap. This scrutiny brings a level of responsibility to the words and actions of established project managers across the field, both in what is said and what is left unsaid.

Project managers are often quite aware of the impression they need to give to their employers, stakeholders, and teams. Project success is dependent on effective communication. However, there are temptations to be aggressive or arrogant in our approaches with others.

The exchange of ideas and perspectives is good, but fruitless combat doesn't only serve no benefit, it leaves the silent observers with an impression of who project managers are that might turn them away. This plays out daily in negative, unhelpful sniping about frameworks, approaches, and even clarification of vocabulary. Those who focus on solutions instead of stewing on problems will be the community-builders of tomorrow's project managers.

On the other hand, many project managers simply opt out of the connectivity and dialogue with their colleagues. They are uninterested or uneasy putting themselves forward and expressing ideas in the open. Not only does this prevent others from learning from their experience and knowledge, but it also loses out on the opportunity to be visible and connect with newcomers, who also might be uncomfortable interacting in a public way. Not every statement needs to be massively public, but being findable and accessible once found are important contributions to the field today.

We are at a crossroads in project management, and I assert that newcomers are going to join the field in large numbers, one way or another. Established project managers owe it to themselves, their organizations, and their colleagues to assist in managing that influx of talent and experience into our field.

The shifting tides toward project management represents a tremendous opportunity for teaching and learning alike. We will be called upon to educate and mentor new project managers, to prime our organizations for future success. However, we can also gain tremendously beneficial knowledge from newcomers who have their own contributions to make in our field. By proactively connecting with these new project managers in organic and authentic ways, we can develop the strength of project management to leverage the knowledge that comes from the combination of our diverse experiences.

CHAPTER NINE

Emotional Intelligence for Project Managers: The Art of Managing Self to Connect with Others

By Jeremiah Hammon

> "Emotion can be the enemy, if you give into your emotion, you lose yourself. You must be at one with your emotions, because the body always follows the mind."- Bruce Lee

Intelligence Quotient (IQ) is a measuring unit for our intelligence potential. It is the Emotional Quotient/Emotional Intelligence (EQ) which makes you socially active and creative.

EQ is the heightened awareness of others' emotions, including your own. The most successful project managers thrive in their respective fields due to their EQ, not IQ. It is an absolute must that leaders in today's corporate world develop their self-awareness, social awareness, and relationship management skills to get the best out of themselves and their team members.

Project managers need to understand themselves at the deepest level so they can understand their team members at the deepest and scientific level. This will allow them to leverage and grow their strengths, skills, personalities, problem solving and decision-making skills, as well as a general EQ baseline so they can formulate a plan and structure the team to perform at its highest.

What exactly is emotional intelligence? Here's a definition:

"The capacity to be aware of, control, and express one's emotions, and to handle interpersonal relationships judiciously and empathetically" (Dictionary.com).

EQ is not only good for your relationship, but also for you and everyone around you!

Crisis Reveals Character

What leadership skills do project managers need? Most of us have worked with or are the technically driven leader, the expert in our field, and we pride ourselves on this. Remember, people will do whatever it takes to maintain consistent with their identity, who they believe they are and how they believe they are supposed to act.

Typically, advancement from this level means entering management, even if managing people is not your area of expertise. Leading and managing teams requires a whole new skillset that must be learned. Without it, you will frustrate your team, your stakeholders, and yourself.

In Salt Lake City, I worked at a bridge crane manufacturing company, steadily advancing in my career. In early 2012, I spotted an opportunity to take on a role as a Project Manager within the company, and I embraced it. I excelled at driving projects to completion, defined by my determination to do whatever was necessary to ensure products moved efficiently in and out the door.

While I was proficient in organizing and scheduling tasks, I had some rough edges. It took a few years of challenges and learning experiences for me to realize a crucial missing piece in my skill set: the ability to understand how I perceived and reacted in stressful situations. This component is a key element of EQ and a vital aspect of great leadership qualities.

My story likely resonates with you or individuals you know, as it's a common one. People are often promoted into leadership roles based on their technical or functional expertise, which enables them to excel in their specific area. However, these promotions sometimes occur without the essential leadership skills needed to inspire, coach, and collaboratively craft a vision that garners commitment, while strengthening ownership and accountability within their teams.

Unfortunately, many organizations fall short in developing their technical performers into well-rounded leaders. Consequently, technical leaders often emulate the behaviors of those who appeared successful before mastering the art of influencing people. Many of these behaviors are reminiscent of past organizational cultures that encouraged authoritarian and autocratic leadership styles. These outdated approaches are ineffective, eroding both performance and well-being within organizations.

The crux of the issue is the lack of clear communication regarding what effective leadership entails in practice, coupled with an absence of structured opportunities for leaders to refine their leadership skills. The gap between leaders' current effectiveness and their untapped potential remains unbridged unless they proactively take charge of their own development and engage in self-education.

This is crucial for everyone to understand. A high level of EQ, especially the competencies of self-awareness and self-control, will define your leadership style and your character.

When there is a lack of EQ in the work environment, particularly in times like now where uncertainty is high and we have to receptive to change. It hampers self-leadership and team leadership, followed by strained communication which leads to disenchanted and disengaged teams. These teams ultimately lose their motivation to think and create effectively, limiting their execution of projects.

Remember this, and commit it to heart: crisis reveals character! If you are unstable in times of crisis, you will lose a lot of respect from your team, peers, and customers, along with the stress it can cause yourself. As the saying goes, "people don't leave bad jobs, they leave bad leaders." If you cannot influence yourself, you cannot influence others and you will not be successful at building high-performing teams.

In the future state of project management, I believe EQ skills will be highly sought-after. Project management professionals will be required to ace far more than the standard project management focus on scope, time, and budget.

The High Cost of Low EQ

Those with low emotional intelligence have several tell-tale signs:

1. They struggle to understand others' feelings and miss social cues that convey emotions.

2. They can't manage their emotions well, leading to exaggerated emotions, poor decision-making, and higher stress levels.

3. They often display inappropriate behavior and speech

due to their lack of emotional intelligence.

4. Empathy and sympathy are challenging for them, making it hard to support others emotionally.
5. They have difficulty being assertive and expressing their wants and needs.
6. Low emotional intelligence results in poor self-control, leading to volatile and impulsive behavior under stress.

EQ is a highly trainable skill. Unlike IQ, it can be improved through education and effort. Some people are born more emotionally intelligent than others, but everyone can learn and develop these important skills. EQ is based on several key skills:

- Self-awareness.
    - ◊ Accurate self-assessment.
    - ◊ Self-confidence.

- Self-management.
    - ◊ Willpower, resilience.
    - ◊ Achievement orientation, standards of excellence.

- Social awareness.
    - ◊ Empathy.
    - ◊ Organizational awareness.

- Relationship management.
    - ◊ Influence.
    - ◊ Leadership.
    - ◊ Communication.

These are key skills for successful project management. By developing their EQ, project managers can build strong relationships with their team members and stakeholders, manage conflict and stress effectively, and motivate and inspire their team members to achieve project goals.

By mastering these four areas, project managers can significantly improve their EQ and their relationships, which will lead to greater success in their projects and careers. My focus in the rest of this chapter will be on self-awareness and self-management.

Mastering Self-Awareness

Self-awareness is a journey of self-discovery. To achieve your goals, you need to know what you truly desire and what drives you. This means aligning your goals with your beliefs and values.

Identify your strengths and weaknesses. If you have any weaknesses that are not essential to your success, don't worry about them. Focus on your strengths and delegate tasks to others.

I had always been ambitious and driven. I always wanted to be the best at whatever I did, and I was always looking for ways to climb the corporate ladder. But my ambition got the better of me. I was so focused on advancing my career that I didn't take the time to develop my leadership skills.

As a result, I made a lot of social mistakes. I was too aggressive and assertive, and I didn't take the time to get to know my team members on a personal level.

One day, I was given the opportunity to lead a new team. I was excited about the challenge, but I quickly realized that I was missing something. I was having a hard time getting people to take ownership of their work. And it was causing conflicts. As leaders, we set the tone. I knew that I needed to change, but I didn't know where to start. I decided to do a self-assessment to identify my strengths and weaknesses. I also started reading books and articles about leadership.

I realized that I needed to develop my self-awareness and self-confidence. I needed to learn how to be a more compassionate and empathetic leader. It took a lot of time and effort, but I eventually made the necessary changes. I became a more effective leader, and my team members started to respect and trust me. I was finally able to create a positive and productive work environment.

I'm still not a perfect leader, but I'm always working on improving. I'm committed to being the leader that my team needs, not the one that I wish I had.

Take an Accurate Self-Assessment

Self-awareness, which is widely recognized as the most important component of EQ, is what we believe. We tend to have a very inaccurate view of ourselves. We can clearly see through the people we know well, but we have a very difficult time seeing ourselves. We deceive ourselves.

Every top project manager or peak performer accurately assesses themselves in order to develop their strengths and understand their limitations. They seek feedback from peers, desire to learn from their mistakes, and know where they need to improve. They also know when to work with others who have complementary strengths that they would like to model.

Peak performers tend to underestimate their abilities, which is a positive sign. People with high standards are always striving to improve.

Develop Your Self-Confidence

Confidence is a learned skill that is closely related to competence. When we are good at something, we are more likely to be confident in our ability to do it well. This confidence can lead to success in a variety of areas, including project management and leadership.

Another vital component of confidence is self-belief. This means believing in our own abilities and worth, even when we make mistakes. It can be difficult to believe in ourselves, especially if we have been told that we are not good enough or if we have experienced setbacks in the past. However, it is important to remember that we are all capable of great things and that we have the potential to achieve our goals.

Demonstrating confidence in the workplace is important for success. In project management and other leadership roles, we interact with many people on a daily basis. How we conduct ourselves demonstrates to those around us what kind of worker and person we are. There will be times when we need to ask others for help. It is during these exchanges that we especially want to show others our confidence in doing our best job possible. Self-awareness is the key to building and maintaining strong relationships.

When you understand how you come across to others, you can communicate more effectively and accurately. Self-awareness helps you understand your emotions and how to manage them, so you take fewer things personally and have a thicker skin.

Self-awareness helps you learn from your mistakes and improve yourself as well as developing the ability to be present in your relationships and notice what's happening with others.

How self-aware are you? It takes a lot of attention and work to know yourself and understand how others view you, but it's worth it for the best relationships possible.

Becoming Self-Aware

How does one become more self-aware? You must be deliberate and courageous. You might not like what you find, but understanding yourself provides the possibility of making positive changes. Your relationship is worth the effort!

Use these strategies to increase your self-awareness and benefit yourself and your relationship:

- **Know your values.** What is important to you in life? Once you know your values, you can start to live a life that is aligned with them.

- **Know your goals.** What do you want your relationship to look like? Once you know your goals, you can start to work towards them.

- **Track your emotions.** Pay attention to how you are feeling and why. This will help you understand your triggers and how to manage your emotions.

- **Take a bird's eye view.** When you have a conflict, try to see the situation from an outsider's perspective. This will help you understand how your actions and words affect others.

- **Review your day.** At the end of each day, take some time to reflect on how you spent your time, what you enjoyed and disliked, and what you learned.

- **Ask a friend for insight.** Ask a trusted friend how others perceive you. This can help you identify areas where you can improve.

Self-awareness is simply paying attention and increasing your understanding of yourself. It is ultimately a habit applied over a long period of time. While it can take years to truly know yourself, you can make huge strides very quickly.

Self-awareness isn't for the weak! It's not always pleasant to learn about yourself. We lie to ourselves so we can salvage a little self-esteem. The truth is that we're naturally oblivious to ourselves. Most of us don't have an accurate opinion of how the world views us.

Knowing yourself will boost your emotional intelligence and enhance your relationship and take you to the next level as a leader.

Mastering Self-Management

You can't manage others unless you're under control. If you do not know what you are feeling you cannot manage your feelings and they manage us weather positive or negative. We are leaders and servants to more we cannot fall victim and be controlled by negative emotions such as frustration, rage, anxiety, and panic.

Self-management or self-regulation is crucial in project management. How you control and manage your emotions, inner resources, and abilities will unlock your ability to manage your behaviors and your reactions to things happening around you. You need to effectively manage stress, control impulses, and motivate yourself.

Self-awareness is crucial for us to know and understand what triggers us. We set the foundation of emotional intelligence which can free us from being held hostage by our emotions. Remember, knowing is not enough and will not get the job done alone. You must do. Take action to regulate yourself.

Self-management is all about controlling the inner conversation and freeing us from being held hostage by our own thoughts, feelings and emotions. Emotions are contagious; we need to be able to manage ourselves to effectively communicate and lead.

This doesn't mean that as a project manager you cannot fall victim to losing your cool. Life has a way to get to us all. It's how we manage our emotions in time of trouble that really shows our character. If we mess up, we fess up, move forward and learn from it by creating strategies to handle those situations better the next go round.

Managing Your Triggers

What happens when we are triggered without awareness of our emotions? We react out of habit and usually in a quick, thoughtless, way. Commit this to heart: Emotional outbursts have public consequences.

Triggers can be caused by events happening in our lives but they can also be activated from remnants of physical and emotional trauma in our past. Our experiences can influence our current perceptions, both positive and negative. Triggers are our hot buttons. You have a strong emotional reaction when it's been pushed.

We have all had an unpleasant experience with a person who looks at you in a certain way or uses a tone that triggers unpleasant feelings. During these encounters you might get instantly upset and react by snapping at them or getting away as fast as you can. In retrospect, you don't not know why but that person's sheer existence upsets you and makes you feel negative.

This situation can happen a lot at work. You may have a boss or coworker that has the same mannerisms as someone from your past. This person from your past impacted you positively or negatively and regularly enough to imbed a reaction to their mannerisms in your subconscious. Someone else talks that way, walks that way, looks a certain way and it can trigger a certain response. These responses are unconscious.

Look to these areas for clues as to what your triggers are: angry, defensive, scared, judging others or ourselves. If you can begin to trace what your triggers are and their causes, you can begin to plan for how to manage them.

Highjacking the Amygdala

We can sometimes feel a "fight or flight" response to our triggers. This reaction was termed "amygdala hijacking" by psychologist Daniel Goleman in his 1995 book, *Emotional Intelligence: Why It Can Matter More Than IQ*. It refers to an immediate and intense emotional reaction that's out of proportion to the situation. In other words, it's when someone "loses it" or seriously overreacts to something or someone.

Goleman's term aims to recognize that we have an ancient primal structure in our brain, the amygdala, that is designed to respond swiftly to a threat. This threat response served humans well while struggling for survival, but it can provide challenges in modern life sometimes. Bursts of intense emotional response might not fit the situation calls for.

If someone threatened your life, then it's appropriate to have a strong emotional response. However, feeling the same emotion in conversation with teammates is a trigger that needs to be recognized, assessed, and managed.

Negative emotions can decrease the brain's capacity to focus on what really matters in our environment. This is why it is so important to know yourself and create tactics to keep you emotions in check. Managing these responses by knowing when they arise and having a plan in place to control them will be the ultimate key to your success. This is the art of Self-management.

To Control or Not to Control?

Self-awareness is the first step to self-management. There are skills you must learn in order to mange yourself at the highest level. Self-control is the ability to choose your emotional or behavioral response to events in your life.

Having self-control allows you to manage your emotions and impulses and use them constructively. By creating a positive path forward, you can maintain your course through chaotic situations. You can stay calm in times of crisis and have a stabilizing effect on the people around you.

Ask yourself these question: Do you know when you are getting frustrated or angry? Do you have the self-control to contain your emotions and control your body language? Can you avoid acting impulsively?

The ability to control your emotions and behavior is a key skill that any leader must learn that allows project managers and teams members to plan, monitor, and attain goals.

You will need both emotional self-control and behavioral self-control. If your ability to control your emotions and behavior are poor, it will have negative consequences on your work performance, relationships, and overall health.

Willpower is a Superpower, But Use Sparingly

The ability to exert self-control is also referred to as willpower. The ability to delay gratification, resisting short-term temptations to meet short- and long-term goals. Self-control is about finding your motivation at the right time. It's about remembering what you truly want so you can do what you must, what you absolutely need to do and resist all the things and temptations you know you shouldn't be doing.

Willpower is like a muscle. It becomes weak with neglect and can get exhausted from non-stop use. If you don't use it, or if you use it too much, you will lose it. We have to exercise care in developing it.

Willpower fluctuates through the day. Our self-control is the highest in the morning and gradually depletes throughout the day with every conscious choice and activity we undertake. We can build our willpower over time if we are committed to doing so, a process that changes our brains right down to the cellular level as we form new habits.

When we think about willpower, most of us think we must be on the defense. We think about seeing the temptation in front of us and we conjure up some willpower to resist it. In most cases we succumb to the temptation because we do not have a plan in place for situations that veer us from our goals.

The most successful people play offense with their willpower. They use self-control to build and establish patterns of excellence. They build habits, plans, and commitments in advance that set them up for success. This can often look like eating healthy, exercising regularly, keeping to a consistent sleep schedule, and abstaining from bad habits. Once a pattern is installed, you will find yourself doing them automatically.

Once you are in the daily groove with your new habits, you will conserve willpower. This means when you need it, you will have it. If an emergency strikes, you will have enough reserves to overcome it.

Avoid temptations, don't just resist them. If you can go on the offensive, you will be far more likely to conserve your willpower, decrease your level of stress and improve your productivity.

Tips to Enhance Your Self-Regulation

Just as you can learn to play an instrument, you can learn to regulate your emotions and behavior. This is a very powerful skill that can make your life better in countless ways. We're often our own worst enemies. Self-regulation allows you to turn yourself into your greatest ally.

Use these tips to learn how to manage your emotions and the resulting behaviors effectively:

- **Meditation and mindfulness.** These are powerful tools for improving self-awareness and self-regulation. Meditation helps you to notice when your attention strays or your emotions are getting off-kilter, while mindfulness helps you to stay in the present moment and observe your thoughts and emotions without judgment.

- **Getting enough sleep and eating a healthy diet.** These are also essential for self-regulation. When you're well-rested and eating nutritious foods, you have more energy and focus, which makes it easier to control your emotions and make good decisions.

- **Exercise.** Another important factor in self-regulation is regular exercise. It reduces stress, improves mood, and increases energy levels.

- **Practice self-soothing and building confidence.** When you feel good about yourself and have healthy ways to cope with negative emotions, you're less likely to act impulsively or react emotionally to situations.

- **Develop self-discipline and a long-term perspective.** This can help you to make good decisions and manage your behavior effectively. Self-discipline allows you to do what you need to do, even when it's difficult, and taking a long-term perspective helps you consider the consequences of your actions before you act.

When you can manage yourself effectively, you open up a whole new world to yourself. You can accomplish much bigger goals and stop sabotaging yourself and your relationship. This is hard work, but worth your effort.

Conclusion

Emotional intelligence is a critical skill for successful project managers. It allows them to lead and motivate their teams, communicate effectively with stakeholders, manage conflict and resolve problems, and create a positive work environment. Project managers can improve their EQ by developing self-awareness, practicing self-regulation, building empathy, and improving social skills. Enhancing these four attributes will allow your relationships to breathe, grow, and reach their full potential.

However, knowledge isn't enough. Make a plan to work on each of those four categories. Start with your weakest area and make some progress before spending your time and attention on one of the other areas.

Personal growth is challenging work, but the rewards are considerable. You're making yourself more powerful and capable when you increase your emotional intelligence. You'll be surprised by how much easier your life and your most important relationships can become.

CHAPTER TEN

Finding the Function in Dysfunction: Trauma's Impact on Project Management Leadership

By Mark Rozner

*G**rowing up, Clark Kent always knew he was a bit different. It didn't feel like a good thing at the time, and he didn't know where it came from. He ultimately learned that he could take on the weight of the world, see through things, even when he shouldn't have been able to, and always moved with a moral imperative.*

He was born into a world where everything had to be perfect but wasn't. He ultimately was pulled away from his family and sent away to live with people who didn't understand him or his ways. It wasn't until he learned of, and worked through, the pain of his early years, that he found his true superpowers.

What does this have to do with project management? Everything! Wouldn't you like to be able to walk into your kickoff meeting and be able to read the room without thinking about it, then control the narrative in the meeting? Would you like to accelerate your stakeholder and risk assessments and the subsequent management activities?

If you grew up in a state of chaos, neglect, or abuse, you have more than likely developed skills that at the time allowed you to cope and even overcome the situation around you. You instinctively know how to match other people's energy, know what someone needs before they even utter a single word, and sense potential failure. What you have overcome is not who you are, nor does it define you but, instead has revealed super-human strengths and aspects that are exceptional and uniquely specific to you.

There are many great resources for helping to transition relevant and related professional skills and experience as you transition into or become a stronger project, program, and portfolio manager, collectively known as P3M or generically, project management. For simplicity when you see references to project management, understand that this can often be applicable to projects, programs, and portfolios.

What doesn't get discussed very often is how to incorporate your past into the needed "soft skills," including emotional intelligence and leadership skills. These soft skills are crucial in the field of project management.

Reviewing my career and how I have managed projects, programs, and portfolios over the past three decades, I can see how I have learned many things over that period, but even more so in the thirty-plus years before that. Previous trauma, especially from childhood (often called Adverse Childhood Experiences (ACEs) or Complex Post Traumatic Stress Disorder (cPTSD)), played a significant role in developing these skills.

While this is not a formal look at childhood trauma including that for any neurological development or long-term mental or physical health impacts, I would like to provide some context. This chapter takes the approach that trauma is something that can be learned from and used positively, rather than be seen as a defect that needs to be accommodated for.

Research indicates that childhood trauma is far more common than one might think. The landmark Adverse Childhood Experiences (ACE) Study conducted by the Centers for Disease Control and Prevention and Kaiser Permanente found that a significant portion of the population had experienced at least one ACE. Trauma can be things that happened to you or things that should have but didn't happen to you. Trauma can typically be traced to your experiences, or those of your parents. Did you or a parent:

- Not get basic emotional needs met consistently?
- Suffer or witness physical abuse or neglect?
- Suffer or witness mental health issues, such as depression or codependency?
- Experience the untimely loss of a parent, child, or other loved one?
- Experience general, yet extended, family dysfunction or chaos?

These and other factors contributed to my own trauma. While this is what I personally experienced, it is not to say that there aren't many other, and potentially far more serious, sources of trauma stemming from negative experiences.

Resolute in the Face of Fear

Trauma shapes your perceptions, coping mechanisms, and emotional regulation. Specifically, trauma can push you to follow a stress and response cycle, often fight or flight. As part of that you, like me, may over time have had these response cycles lead to so many negative behaviors:

- Elevated fear, including feeling like an imposter in your own life

- Decreased trust, leading to an elevated need for control

- Setting unachievable goals and values for yourself, ultimately doing the same for others

- Unhealthy levels of people pleasing

These and other factors may have found you developing specific coping mechanisms and tools to make daily life in school, work, and relationships bearable. Going forward you can learn how to compensate or mitigate the effects and even turn them into strengths and opportunities for self-growth: effectively taking the "bad" and turning it "good."

The bottom line is that your childhood informs your way of thinking and interacting with the world around you. For many of us, if you peel back all the layers what you find is fear. You will need to find your way to work through those fears. You will need to find an instinct that is simpler and more powerful than fear itself.

This is about making the fear and pain, the uncertainty, and the doubt which built up over those formative years as impactful as any class you can take or certifications you can accumulate.

My path included generating a personal manifesto, a written statement to declare my intentions, motivations, and beliefs. Effectively, I created a set of agreements with myself, like The Five Agreements as written by members of the Ruiz family.

I started with what I love:

- The sights and sounds of water running free.
- Cool wind on my warm skin.
- Unexpected encounters with nature.
- The right sound or song at the right time.
- Holding hands with someone I care about.
- To be challenged intellectually.

Continued with what I believe...

- There is no evil, only pain.
- There is that which can be explained by science and faith for when it cannot.

And finally, what I am committed to...

- Live with intention.
- Act with integrity, courage, and grace, a litmus test for any major decisions.
- Find my why, passion, goals.
- Listen hard.
- Accumulate nothing but experiences and memories.
- Always stop to smell the roses.
- Continue to learn.

I committed to learning how to:

- Practice wellness.
- Play and laugh with abandon.
- Love unconditionally.
- Believe in my true worth.
- Choose without regret.
- Appreciate both failure and success; not to be afraid of either.
- No longer sabotage myself personally, or professionally.

This is what I came up with for me – take the time and space to document your own manifesto!

Once you have begun to find who you are and what traits you want to expand on, you need to clearly articulate and document the strengths you want to demonstrate and the areas you want to improve. Do you need to find your self-motivation and sufficiency? Enhance your communications skills? Advocate for yourself and others? Set and assert your own boundaries? Prioritize wellbeing?

From Weakness to Strength

Strength doesn't always mean completely overcoming the impact; it can also be learning to live despite it. I have taken the lessons and mechanisms learned living in a family filled with chaos and trauma and found ways to make them into my P3M superpowers.

The skills we learned to survive trauma are the same that

can make us powerful project management leaders:

- Our want for peace in our environment drives us to be the helper and mediator.

- We make use of inclusive and often-times ethical decision-making, we push to understand, and we use this to manage our stakeholders' needs.

- We use our developed strength and resilience to bring our efforts to fruition, with a positive result.

- The creativity we built to handle our traumas now pushes us to ensure that our projects, programs, and portfolios, at the very least, consider growth, innovation, and ultimately sustainability .

- During execution we use this same capability to problem-solve, sometimes at moment's notice and with only the knowledge we possess at that moment. We take that information, put it into perspective, add in our empathy, and move to consider the solutions and outcomes.

While looking back on the hardships of your traumas might feel uncomfortable, finding meaning in them can be quite enriching. As an example, people with parents suffering from mental illness mention that their experience taught them:

- Empathy and compassion towards those in pain.
- Appreciation for moments of peace and simplicity.
- Resilience in the face of adversity.

Shifting your perspective from what caused damage and negativity, towards your inner strength and positivity, helps accept your past and work with it, not against it.

Making the Way Forward

Trauma isn't something you can just "get over" with a snap of your fingers. Recovery, as a rule, involves a number of tasks to work through, and you can't really skip any of them.

First, focus on self (both self-awareness and self-management). They say the first step is realizing you have a problem, so let's start there. To grow you must first learn, to learn you must first identify. The process to do this isn't quick, easy, or painless.

One way to approach this is to use your own project management skills, specifically risk and stakeholder management. You will need to evaluate your strengths, weaknesses, opportunities, and threats (SWOT). What do you bring? What needs to be compensated for, mitigated, or turned into an opportunity?

This takes much time, work, and the help, support, and counseling of others (including mental health professionals). It could include exploring spirituality, mindfulness, meditation, or other strategies. That said, this chapter is not meant to be a primer on self-help, metaphysics, or religion, although those can help in some cases.

During all of this please keep in mind that you will go through several stages of self-awareness, contemplation, preparation, action, integration, and maintenance. There are many models for this, like what you would see written about for stages of grief and recovery. Please also keep in mind that much like projects are not just linear, you may find yourself having to take a step back and iterate through one or more stages. Just remember to capture your lessons learned at each stage.

Trauma may affect our brains in a negative way, but trauma can also lead to enormous growth, resilience, and empowerment, sometimes called post-traumatic growth (PTG).

PTG refers to positive psychological changes or personal development that can occur in the aftermath of a traumatic or challenging experience. Unlike traditional views of trauma that focus solely on negative outcomes, PTG suggests that individuals can undergo positive transformations because of their struggle with adversity.

PTG can involve:

- New possibilities.
    - ◊ Meeting new psychological needs.
    - ◊ Living life differently than before the trauma.

- Increased personal strength / growth.
    - ◊ Developing beyond one's previous functioning level.

- Enhanced relationship (to others).
    - ◊ Forging new relationships.
    - ◊ Being more grateful for existing relationships.

- Appreciation of life.
    - ◊ Taking new meaning from experiences.

- Spiritual/religious growth.
    - ◊ Creating new belief systems.

PTG doesn't deny the distress of trauma, but rather suggests that adversity can lead to changes in how one understands oneself, others, and the world in general.

EQ and Leadership

Much is talked about what differentiates a "leader" from a "boss" in personal management of individuals and teams. As I touched on above, the same is true for project managers and project leaders. There is much discussion on this, online, in journals, and by any number of experts. So, the question is, what makes that difference. I see this as dependence on use of Emotional Intelligence (EQ).

For over thirty years, EQ has become a catch-all for what might be thought of as overall consideration and intentional thinking. Interestingly, you will find it synonymous with emotional regulation, looking at controlling yourself and others, based upon a larger understanding. I prefer to look at it less as control and more as identification, comprehension, and the ability to override one's own and others' governance, sentiment, perceptions, and viewpoints.

A big piece of EQ is about knowing your values and truly being authentic. When confronted with a seemingly tough decision, revisiting your values can make the decision suddenly and almost surprisingly straightforward. Values are like an internal rudder steering us through a life of decisions.

Using emotional intelligence to inform your decisions means being aware of what you are feeling when weighing your choices. It also means being aware of how others will feel based on the decisions you make. Being emotionally intelligent means asking yourself, "Are my emotions helping or hindering me here? Will other people feel like helping me or hindering me?"

A deeper dive on EQ itself has been covered by Jeremiah Hammon in a previous chapter, but I bring it up here, as it is a conduit between what you take from your post-traumatic growth and move into your leadership and PM superpowers.

Specifically, the components of EQ translate and connect to components of leadership:

- Leaders who are **self-aware** understand how their emotions affect their team's performance
- Leaders who can **self-regulate** can recognize their emotions and modify their behavior
- Leaders with high emotional intelligence are **motivated** and can inspire others
- Leaders who are **empathetic** can understand and relate to the emotions of others
- Leaders with good **social skills** can build relationships and work well with others. This includes team cooperation, conflict resolution, inspiration, guidance, support, and last but not least, stakeholder management

EQ Applied in Project Management

While EQ has been studied for many years now, we don't find its relationship to project management documented until 2013, when it was identified as a possible indicator of job performance for construction project managers. At the time a direct link between EQ and project management practices such as leadership, communication, and relationship building was made.[1]

In building emotional intelligence capabilities, you can move your role from managing scope, schedule, and resource

---

[1] Zhang, Lianying & Fan, Weijie. (2013). Improving performance of construction projects: A project manager's emotional intelligence approach. *Engineering, Construction and Architectural Management*, 20(2), 195-207. https://doi.org/10.1108/09699981311303044

to looking at the risk, quality, and ultimately the value that your project will deliver. As you expand this view you can take advantage of this by moving from "Command and control" to "engage, connect and align," two contrasting approaches to organizational leadership and management. These concepts reflect different paradigms in how leaders interact with their teams and guide organizational processes.

Command-and-Control

The "command-and-control" approach is characterized by a hierarchical structure where leaders exert authority and make decisions that are then implemented by subordinates. It involves a top-down flow of information and strict adherence to established procedures.

Leaders using this approach tend to be directive, focusing on clear instructions and strict supervision. Decisions often originate at the top levels of the hierarchy and are communicated downward.

Communication in a command-and-control structure is typically one-way, with information flowing from leaders to subordinates. Feedback may be limited, and decisions are centralized.

This concept has roots in traditional management theories, such as Frederick Taylor's scientific management principles. It is associated with a more authoritarian leadership style and is often criticized for stifling creativity and adaptability.

Engage, Connect, and Align

The "engage, connect, and align" approach emphasizes collaboration, employee engagement, and alignment of individual and organizational goals. Leaders focus on building relationships, fostering open communication, and aligning team members with the organization's vision.

Leaders using this approach are often facilitative and participative. They seek input from team members, encourage collaboration, and aim to create a positive organizational culture.

Communication in this approach is bi-directional, with a focus on open dialogue and feedback. Team members are encouraged to express their ideas and contribute to decision-making processes.

This approach aligns with contemporary leadership theories, including transformational leadership and servant leadership. Scholars like Daniel Pink, in his book Drive, emphasize the importance of autonomy, mastery, and purpose in motivating individuals and teams.

"Command and control" is often associated with traditional project management practices, while "engage, connect, and align" is associated with more contemporary and people-centric project leadership philosophies. Moving from the former to the latter is aided by using our trauma-informed capabilities.

Project Manager vs. Project Leader

Even when starting out in project management, you should look to manage more than just the project. You should aim to be seen as a project leader. Project managers generally have accountability and responsibility for project efforts but typically aren't given the needed authority or even influence that would support their success. At a minimum, this requires you to find someone who has authority to proxy that authority to you. Ultimately, you need to be seen as that trusted advisor who should be given the authority to secure the success of the project's efforts.

A project leader has more focus on the people and "soft skills" rather than the more technical aspects of a given project. Soft skills reflect a person's relationship with other people through his or her character traits and interpersonal skills. A person with good interpersonal skills focuses more on who people are, rather than what they know. It makes the work environment easier to manage, often through subtle behaviors and communication.

Trauma informs our emotional intelligence, leadership, and interpersonal skills. These, in turn, influence our abilities to perform as project leaders, including the following areas:

- **Scope management.** As P3M leaders we want to see our efforts bring the desired value to the organization. It isn't enough to expect project deliverables, but also product deliverables. We must look to our need for the product development to make use of creativity and consider long-term sufficiency and sustainability.

- **Risk and benefits management.** Trauma creates an overabundance of need to control situations. This takes many forms in P3M. The first is the want to mitigate unintended consequences and ultimately, minimize harm.

- **Communication, decision-making, and change management.** Trauma informed project management leaders will look to proactively address communication, decision-making, and change management, putting them together into comprehensive frameworks.

If you can mediate chaos as a child with those tools, think what you can do with them when working with that "one" stakeholder standing in the way of success. That feeling you had as a child walking into a room and not knowing what was going to happen between you and the person responsible for your care, has given you the gift of walking into a meeting and "reading the room." When you as a child found yourself comforting the adults around you, you learned how to empathize without the benefit of being able to sympathize.

Conclusion

It is far too easy to let the events of our childhood be a reason to fail in life. What isn't easy is taking the time and energy to find ways to take that experience and make it our reason for success in life. Put in the time, put in the energy, learn about who you are now, determine what is important to you now, and decide to prioritize your personal growth, your learning, and your well-being.

When you begin to process your traumas and start the healing process, lean into what those experiences taught you about self-awareness, self-management, and communication. Take the tools you will have built to manage and mitigate your thoughts, feelings, and environment, and put them in the same toolbox as your other project management tools.

Note: I am not a mental health professional and this information should not be considered medical advice. Please see your doctor if you have any concerns about your own mental health. Remember to take care of yourself!

Afterword

Every book contains the echo of a voice, or in this case, a group of voices. The authors who have contributed to this work have tremendously varied backgrounds and experiences in the field of project management.

These project professionals are all noteworthy for their dedication to assisting those around them in their project management communities. They strive to demonstrate a spirit of mentorship and learning in equal measure. They come to each problem in search of solutions to supply.

Despite the varied backgrounds of all involved in this endeavor, it is clear in retrospect that there are themes that emerge in these reflections. Themes of emotional intelligence and personal well-being, development of career, use of tools both new and established, and a focus on community learning are woven throughout this work.

It is obvious to most observers that these themes reflect the state of our profession in a world that has never had more opportunities nor presented so many challenges for project managers than ever before. At the time of publication, project management projects to go through the same massive demographic shifts as reflected in the rest of the world's workforce.

New generations of workers often demand new approaches to leadership, challenging established paradigms in workplaces across the globe. The rise of AI tools has rocked perceptions of what it means to perform project work, both worrying skeptics and intriguing users with the offer of unrivaled efficiency and power.

It is impossible to predict what the future will bring, but many project managers stand ready to rise to the challenges we may face. Project managers have established a well-deserved reputation as problem-solvers. The fact that many are so willing to help one another gives hope that this ability will serve our profession well.

About the Authors

Chapter One: Solving the Paradox of Project Success

After he graduated in 1978, **Adrian Dooley** moved into construction project management and thought that would be his career. In 1979, a very happy accident resulted in his being part of a team that developed one of the first project planning software packages for the new 'Microcomputers.' It was taken up by Apple and became 'Apple Project Manager.' Adiran was hooked and went back to University on a research project to develop more construction applications.

After a return to the construction project management coalface, he struck out on my own. It was the best decision he ever made and he ended up training and consulting on all things project management in numerous industries for over 25 years.

Along the way, Adrian and some friends started the first independent project management magazine and exhibition. He served on the Council of the Association of Project Management (APM) and remains a non-executive Director of APMGroup, that kicked off the PRINCE2 certification scheme.

After retirement, Adrian was lead author for the 6th edition of the APM Body of Knowledge and subsequently created the Praxis Framework. He has now come full circle with AI being as revolutionary today as microcomputers were nearly 45 years ago. It's been a fun journey.

Chapter Two: Freelancing and Project Management

Kayla McGuire is a trusted strategic advisor, enthusiastic project management coach, and the founder of Kayla McGuire Consulting, LLC. For the past 15 years, Kayla has worked with entrepreneurs to launch and scale start-up operations. With experience that spans disciplines, Kayla is known for her ability to form and execute visionary plans without sacrificing agility or compromising the team's wellbeing, which she credits to a deep understanding of project management fundamentals.

Kayla's background in business building helped make it a natural move when it came time to embark on her freelancing career in 2020. Through her consulting company, she has built and executed project management training programs, coached dozens of project managers as they launch their freelancing careers, and advised founders on operational strategy and project best practices, leading to growth and scale. Additionally, her e-book "The Freelance Project Manager Guide Book" has served as a blueprint for aspiring freelancers worldwide.

Beyond her consulting work, Kayla shares her passion for project management on her YouTube channel as well as LinkedIn. Her original content closes the gap between the technical knowledge needed to excel as a project manager and the day to day reality of life as a freelancer.

Kayla lives in Bentonville, AR with her daughter and their lovable canine companion, Murray. Learn more about her work at www.kaylamcguire.com.

Chapter Three: Tech-Forward Project Management: Mastering the Digital Landscape

Dr. Tori R. Dodla is a professional in the realm of information technology and knowledge management. She has excelled in spearheading collaborative projects, particularly focusing on Microsoft 365 platform solutions. Her responsibilities have often encompassed developing migration strategies, streamlining knowledge management processes, and mentoring teams in complex technological environments.

As an educator, Dr. Dodla has imparted her extensive knowledge in various subjects including Advanced Database Systems, Information Systems, and Object Oriented Programming. In addition, her authorship in esteemed publications reflects her thought leadership in her field. Her articles on knowledge management strategies are a testament to her research skills and deep understanding of the subject.

Dr. Dodla holds a Doctor of Philosophy in Information Technology which was built upon a solid foundation of a Master's degree in Management Information Systems and a Bachelor's degree in Funeral Service. She holds an array of professional certifications, demonstrating her commitment to continuous learning and staying updated with the latest trends and advancements in her field. These include credentials in knowledge management, security fundamentals, and project management, among others.

Chapter Four: Project Manager Authority and the Affect It Has on Project Manager Stress

Dr. Max Boller has distinguished himself over a 15-year career in project and program management across the Information Technology, hospitality, and retail sectors. He has excelled in roles from project manager to director of operations, exemplifying adaptability and deep expertise. Currently, as Senior Project Manager at Dairy Queen, a part of Berkshire Hathaway, he adeptly aligns and executes strategic initiatives, ensuring they meet the company's goals.

Academically, Dr. Boller is highly credentialed, holding a Doctor of Business Administration specializing in project management, a Post-master's Certificate in the discipline, and a Master of Business Administration. His academic prowess is complemented by certifications as a Project Management Professional and a Scrum Master, demonstrating his ability to blend traditional and agile methodologies effectively.

In addition to his professional duties, Dr. Boller is passionate about research, focusing on the psychological impacts of project management, such as stress and burnout. He aims to illuminate and mitigate these issues, striving to balance professional success with mental well-being. His work is a testament to his commitment to not only advancing project management practices but also enhancing the health and welfare of those in the field.

Chapter Five: De Facto vs. De Jure Projects

Joseph Jordan has been up and down the ladder of success a few times over his forty-plus year career. He's done everything from Cold-War warrior in the U.S. Navy to working as a waiter in an Italian restaurant – in Italy!

Besides Italy, he has lived in Turkey, Germany, Bosnia–Herzegovina, and many states within the U.S. Between 2006 and 2016, he spent a total of six full years "boots on the ground" in Afghanistan over several deployments. During this time he was put in charge of IT enterprise programs and led numerous IT infrastructure projects for the U.S. Department of Defense.

He returned to the U.S. for good in 2017 with Trace Systems, an organization he helped grow from a one-contract company to a respected, medium-sized defense contractor with over 300 employees deployed across five continents with 1.2 billion dollars' worth of programs.

He has accumulated numerous Microsoft Windows administration certifications, achieved the CISSP in 2009, the PMP in 2013, and a BS in IT Systems – also in 2013 – at the age of 53.

Since 2022, he has been writing at www.josephjordan.org and on LinkedIn at www.linkedin.com/in/josephjordanpmp about project and program management.

Chapter Six: Good Communication Practices Throughout the Project Lifecycle

Walt Sparling works as project management leader, managing a team of project managers in the construction industry for an international professional services firm in the real estate space.

Walt's background includes more than thirty years on the design and project management side of the building industry that included HVAC, electrical, plumbing, and architecture.

A major focus of Walt's work has been finding and implementing ways to reduce complexity, save time, review standards, and create better documentation processes. This work led Walt to start a website and podcast focused on project management and helping project managers grow and master their project management skills.

You can find more about Walt on LinkedIn at https://www.linkedin.com/in/waltsparling/ and on the PM Mastery website at https://PM-Mastery.com.

Chapter Seven: From Manager to Leader: Unboxing the Power of Value-Based Performance and Personal Branding

Known to speak from the heart with a dash of sassy, **Tareka Wheeler** is an effective thought-provoking storyteller, who uses her own personal and professional journey to teach and empower others. Whether she is teaching organizations how to develop a strategic plan or is presenting to professionals on how to advance in their careers without sacrificing work-life harmony, Tareka brings energy, vision, and wisdom to every conversation so individuals can walk in their authentic power and begin to see countless opportunities to evolve.

With a career that spans nearly 20 years, Tareka is a distinguished expert in program and project management and is a career and work-life strategist. Leveraging many core project management principles and methods, she has worked alongside Fortune 400 and 500 companies, federal agencies, and non-profits to deliver impactful outcomes in the fields of public health, strategic communications and information technology.

Tareka earned her bachelor's from St. Edward's University in Organizational Communication and has her PMP.

Chapter Eight: Lessons from Outside: Infinite Diversity in Infinite Combinations

John Connolly is a project management consultant and author. A veteran of the information management field, he has worked in software, libraries, for government agencies, and as a contracted specialist in data and information management.

John's focus is on the application of information management principles and practices in project management to facilitate the sharing of knowledge across the project management community. With an emphasis on collecting and sharing these critical lessons learned, he has worked to build community and collaboration with project managers across many industries.

He is the founder of Salientian, a project management training and consultation company. He is also the founder and Editor-in-Chief of Community Milestone Press, a publisher of project management books.

Connect with John on LinkedIn at https://www.linkedin.com/in/johnconnolly058/ or at https://www.salientian.com.

Chapter Nine: Emotional Intelligence for Project Managers: The Art of Managing Self to Connect with Others

Jeremiah Hammon is the author of *The Project Management Pathway*, a transformative guide forged from 15 years of navigating the complex industries of aerospace, nuclear energy, and civil engineering.

Recognizing a critical void in project management, he focuses on crucial yet often overlooked productivity and soft skills. His programs and book go beyond standard methodologies to cover leadership, emotional/social intelligence, organizational awareness, agility, and resilience.

Jeremiah's business, Project Revolution, is on a mission to ignite a wildfire within 2,000 visionary businesses, empowering them to lead the charge in reshaping and changing our world, and he will stop at nothing to ensure their success.

His vision revolves around creating a high-voltage culture of top-talent rock stars who love what they do, know who they do it for, how they do it, and why they do it. To unlock the greatest asset of every business, people, propelling business owners towards purpose, high performance, and unparalleled achievement.

Jeremiah is available via email at team@projectrevolutionllc.com and you can connect with him on LinkedIn at
https://www.linkedin.com/in/jeremiahrhammonjr/

Chapter Ten: Finding the Function in Dysfunction: Trauma's Impact on Project Management Leadership

Mark Rozner Mark Rozner has over four decades of leadership experience in highly visible and complex health care, financial services, and other corporate support organizations.

A veteran of the United States Air Force, Mark served in the medical field, and in the process, gained insights into holistic patient care and seeing first-hand the effect of streamlining patient processes. Combining his love for technology and passion for healthcare, Mark went on to work for national and international software vendors, implementing clinical and financial healthcare information systems. His roles evolved from subject matter expert to project manager and included working in the financial and other sectors.

He founded Sunrise Path LLC in 2018, a continuation of his passion for transforming how healthcare is delivered and shaping the craft of project management. Recently semi-retired, he dedicates much of his time and energy into transferring his knowledge to future generations through mentoring, regularly contributing to online communities, and serving as an advisor to a project management SaaS system provider.

An active member of the Project Management Institute since 2003, receiving his PMP Certification. He also has certifications in change acceleration and quality management.

Connect with Mark on LinkedIn at
https://www.linkedin.com/in/markrozner/

Made in United States
Orlando, FL
07 February 2025